Dinosaurs

AND OTHER
PREHISTORIC
LIFE

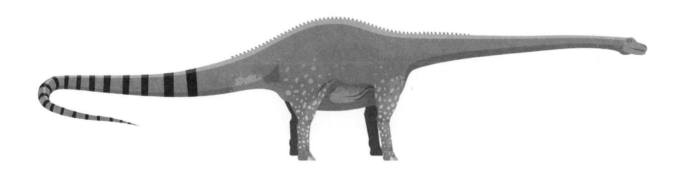

Written by Professor Anusuya Chinsamy-Turan

Illustrated by Angela Rizza
and Daniel Long

Introduction

Are you ready for an amazing expedition that starts at the beginning of life on Earth? In this book, you will see how the earliest life-forms developed in water, and how much later plants and then animals moved onto land. You will encounter weird and wonderful prehistoric creatures that will challenge your imagination, including fearsome fish, gigantic insects, and, yes, dinosaurs galore! Further on, you will learn what became of dinosaurs and their descendants, and how mammals came to dominate our planet. Finally, as our voyage draws to a close, you will meet early human relatives and see the animals that lived alongside them. Come, let's begin…

Professor Anusuya Chinsamy-Turan
Author

Contents

Paleozoic Era

541–252 Million Years Ago (MYA)

Earth is over 4.5 billion years old. To try and make sense of this immense time, scientists divide it up into chunks. For much of the first 4 billion years, known as the Precambrian, only microscopic life existed. Familiar animals began to appear at the beginning of the Phanerozoic Eon, which is divided into three big eras: the Paleozoic, Mesozoic, and Cenozoic. The Paleozoic Era lasted 289 million years, and it is split into six different periods: the Cambrian, Ordovician, Silurian, Devonian, Carboniferous, and Permian. This era featured an explosion of different life-forms, first in the oceans and then on land.

Devonian Period (419–358 MYA)

More and more plants and insects appeared on land during the Devonian. Toward the end of the period, the first animals with four legs crawled onto land and forests covered the ground. This period ended with a second mass extinction event.

Carboniferous Period (358–298 MYA)

In the Carboniferous, the continents moved even closer together. The southern regions were covered with ice, but there were also plenty of tropical forests. Some amphibians gave rise to the first reptiles.

Cambrian Period (541-485 MYA)

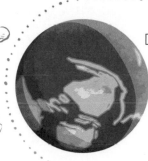

During the Cambrian, several different landmasses were gathered in the southern hemisphere of the Earth. In the ocean, there was a rapid increase in the different types of animals, which is often referred to as "The Cambrian Explosion."

Ordovician Period (485-443 MYA)

In the Ordovician, plants began to adapt to living on land, rather than in water. However, by the end of the period huge ice sheets spread over the continents, which led to a mass extinction event.

Silurian Period (443-419 MYA)

Earth's continents began to move together in the Silurian, and life slowly recovered from the mass extinction event. During this period, taller land plants started to grow, and arthropods moved onto land.

Permian Period (298-252 MYA)

By the Permian Period, the continents had merged into a supercontinent, called Pangea. More types of reptile evolved, and the ancestors of mammals appeared, but the period ended with the biggest mass extinction event of all time.

Stromatolite

Stromatolites (stroh-MA-toh-lites) might look like big boulders, but they are no ordinary rocks. They are among the world's oldest fossils, which were formed by microscopic organisms called cyanobacteria, or blue-green algae. As they grew, the cyanobacteria formed slimy mats that trapped grains of soil and sand, which solidified into rocks. Stromatolite-forming cyanobacteria can still be found today, but only in a few places around the world. They like to make their home in very salty water, where other animals cannot live—and cannot eat them!

More than 3.4 billion years ago, cyanobacteria began to photosynthesize, like plants do today, putting oxygen into the atmosphere of the planet. This allowed many more oxygen-breathing creatures to appear.

Stromatolite. Precambrian to present, Worldwide. This slice through a 2.4-billion-year-old stromatolite shows the layers formed as the cyanobacteria grew.

Dickinsonia was soft-bodied, so only
impressions of it are found as fossils.

Dickinsonia

I t may be hard to believe, but this flat, leaflike organism was
actually an animal! We know this because cholesterol—a type
of fat found only in animals—has been identified in Dickinsonia
(dickin-SO-nee-a) fossils. This creature lived around 567 million
years ago and is one of the world's oldest known animals, although
scientists disagree about what type of animal it was.

How did it move? How did it grow? There is still much we do
not understand about this puzzling life-form. Curiously, no mouth
or gut can be identified in Dickinsonia, which suggests that it may
have moved along the seafloor and absorbed food through the
underside of its soft body.

**Dickinsonia. Precambrian, Asia,
Europe, and Oceania.** This fossil
impression of Dickinsonia shows
the central ridge that divided the
animal into a right and left half.

Anomalocaris. Cambrian Period, Asia, North America, and Oceania. This fossil shows one of Anomalocaris's long spiked mouthparts.

Anomalocaris

When fossils of the different body parts of Anomalocaris (a-NOM-a-low-CAR-iss) were discovered, scientists were convinced that they belonged to different animals. Its circular mouth was thought to be a jellyfish and its long mouthparts were mistaken for shrimp! Eventually though, it became clear that they were all parts of a single incredible animal—Anomalocaris. This enormous early arthropod, related to crustaceans and insects, lived in the ocean and grew up to 3 ft (1 m) long.

Anomalocaris existed more than 500 million years ago. To swim, it flapped the flattened sides of its body like wings, allowing it to glide through the water. Anomalocaris's two long, curved mouthparts were lined with vicious spikes—perfect for skewering squishy prey.

Anomalocaris was the largest animal of its time, and the first top predator on Earth.

The Cambrian Explosion

The Cambrian Explosion was the sudden increase in different life-forms around 541 million years ago, during the Cambrian Period. Before the Cambrian Explosion, only a few large animals existed on Earth, but from that time on, there were all sorts of creatures. Exactly what caused this rapid "explosion" of different types of life is uncertain. It is possible that the increase in oxygen in the atmosphere may have let animals grow bigger, or changes in their DNA may have allowed them to evolve into new shapes. Here you can see some of the wonderful animals that lived at that time.

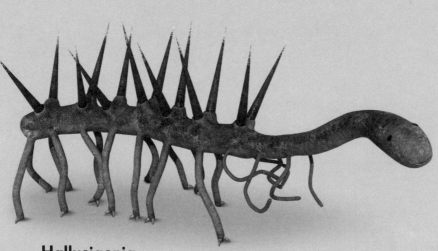

Hallucigenia
Hallucigenia (ha-lucy-JEAN-ee-a) was a bizarre, wormlike animal that had thin legs to walk and spines along its back. Its fossils are well-known in Cambrian rocks from a fossil site called the Burgess Shale, in Canada.

Wiwaxia

Spiny Wiwaxia (we-WAX-ee-a) lived at the bottom of the sea. It was protected by hard plates and long spikes. Scientists aren't sure, but it may have been a mollusk, related to snails.

Haikouichthys

A small, fishlike animal, Haikouichthys (HIGH-koo-IK-this) was special because it had a distinct head and the beginnings of a backbone. It is considered an early relative of all vertebrates (animals with a backbone).

Opabinia

Odd-looking Opabinia (OH-pa-BIN-ee-a) was a soft-bodied animal equipped with long mouthparts ending in a claw that it probably used to grab prey. Stranger still, it had five eyes on its head!

Anomalocaris

The vicious-looking Anomalocaris (a-NOM-a-low-CAR-iss) lurked in the Cambrian ocean. It was a giant predator with two huge eyes and spiked mouthparts. Anomalocaris fossils have been found in the Burgess Shale fossil site in Canada.

Hallucigenia

Hallucigenia (ha-lucy-JEAN-ee-a) looked a bit like a worm on stilts, but when it was discovered in the 1970s it confused paleontologists. What type of animal was it? An arthropod, like an insect, or perhaps a relative of modern velvet worms? It is still not certain. Even figuring out what Hallucigenia looked like was tricky. Which way up did it stand? And which end was its head? New fossils of this 510-million-year-old creature show that it had up to 10 pairs of legs and seven pairs of pointed spines on its back. Hallucigenia's semicircular mouth was surrounded by small teeth, but it also had teeth lining its throat! It probably ate by sucking up its food, which was shredded on the way to its stomach.

Hallucigenia was given its name, which means "wandering of the mind," because it looked so bizarre.

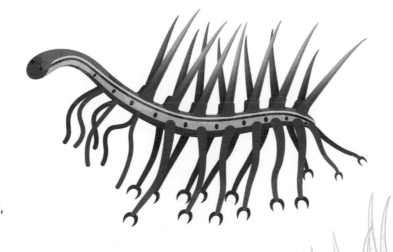

Hallucigenia. Cambrian Period, Asia and North America. In this fossil, Hallucigenia's head can be seen on the left and the straight spikes on its back are above.

Cooksonia

Cooksonia (COOK-so-NEE-ah) didn't have any leaves, flowers, or roots, but it was still a plant! It was one of the first plants to have a strong stem to support it—earlier plants lived in the water or grew in low mats on the ground. Cooksonia's branching green stems may have also used a process called photosynthesis to harvest energy from the sun.

From the fossils we've found, we know only what Cooksonia looked like in one stage in its life cycle—when it was about to reproduce by releasing seedlike spores. At that point, oval-shaped spore factories, called sporangia, had formed at the tips of its stems. What Cooksonia looked like the rest of the time is still a mystery.

Cooksonia was one of the first
plants to grow on land.

Cooksonia. Silurian to Devonian periods, Worldwide. The cuplike shapes at the top of this fossil are the sporangia, where spores were made.

The state fossil of New York is *Eurypterus remipes*—a type of *Eurypterus* that is commonly found there.

Eurypterus

Eurypterus (you-RIP-terruss) was unlike any creature alive today. It belonged to a group of animals called eurypterids, also known as "sea scorpions" because of their sharp tail spines. Eurypterus crawled along the bottom of Silurian seas more than 400 million years ago, hunting for prey to seize with its spiny arms. Fossilized Eurypterus droppings contain clues to what it ate—the remains of trilobites, fish, and even other eurypterids have been found inside them! Its rear pair of legs were paddlelike, and Eurypterus used them to swim quickly, but it could walk on the seafloor, too. As it grew, Eurypterus shed its hard outer shell from time to time, and the remains of these shells sometimes became fossilized.

Eurypterus. Silurian Period, North America. The segmented shell of Eurypterus fit together like a suit of armor.

Australaster

This sea star almost looks as if it could crawl off its rock, but it is around 430 million years old! Australaster (OSS-tra-last-er) lived in the Silurian Period, but the first sea stars, which appeared in the Cambrian, looked remarkably similar to their relatives today. Sea stars are echinoderms (ee-KYE-no-derms)— a group of animals that also includes sea urchins, brittle stars, and the extinct blastoids— all of which have hard outer coverings.

Sea stars creep along the bottom of the seafloor using their tentacle-like tube feet to walk. These stick out of grooves that run in a line along the underside of each arm. At the center of these grooves is a circular mouth. Prehistoric sea stars probably used it to gobble up sponges and other invertebrates on the seabed.

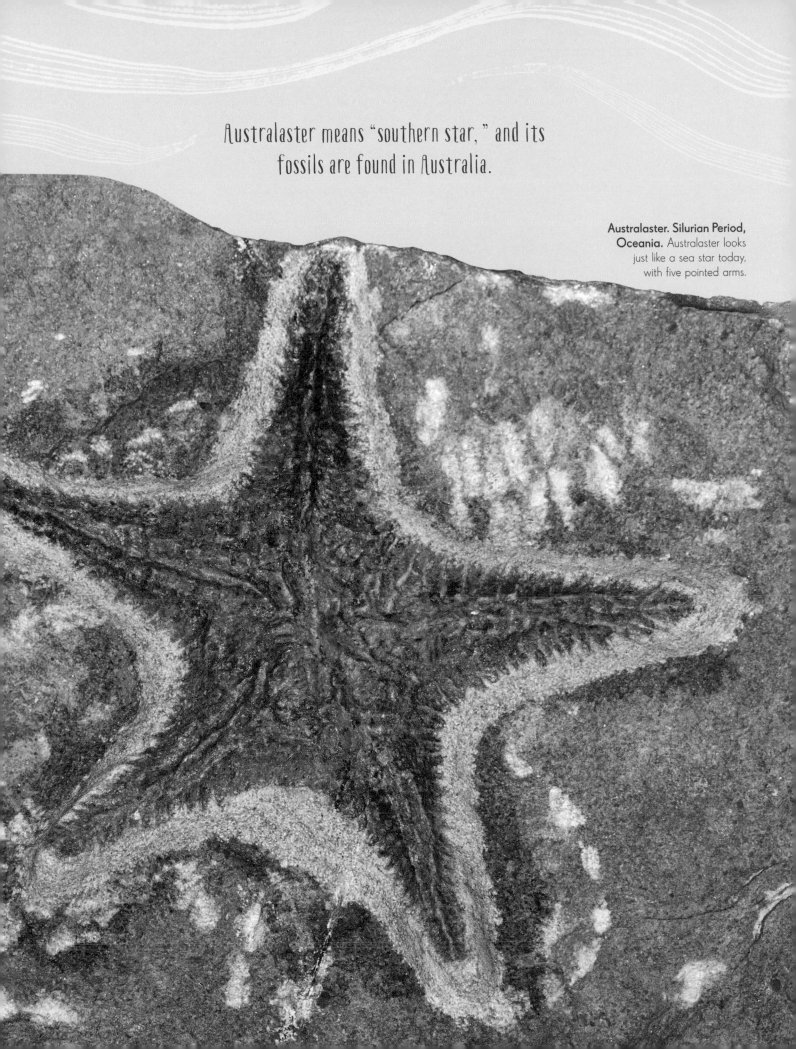

Australaster means "southern star," and its fossils are found in Australia.

Australaster. Silurian Period, Oceania. Australaster looks just like a sea star today, with five pointed arms.

Cephalaspis

Cephalaspis might have been able to detect electricity,
like a shark can, to help it find prey.

Cephalaspis. Devonian Period, Europe and North America.
Cephalaspis could grow to about 10 in (25 cm) long. This body fossil shows the head shield on the left.

Coasting over the bottom of the ocean around 400 million years ago, Cephalaspis (SEFF-a-LASP-iss) lived during the Devonian Period. It was a type of jawless fish, which meant that it didn't have hinged jaws for chewing food. Instead, Cephalaspis would have simply vacuumed up invertebrates from the seafloor using a mouth hidden on the underside of its head.

Cephalaspis had a tough covering over its curved head. In fact, its name means "head shield" in ancient Greek—an aspis was a wooden shield carried by ancient Greek soldiers. This armor helped protect Cephalapsis from bigger fish and sea scorpions looking for a snack!

Tower-eyed trilobites could see all around, even backward over their bodies.

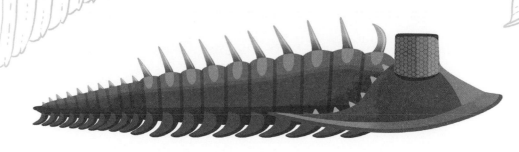

Erbenochile

Erbenochile (er-BEN-oh-CHILL-ee) looked a little like a prehistoric woodlouse, but it was, in fact, a trilobite, which crawled around the ocean. Trilobites were arthropods—the group including spiders, insects, and woodlice—but their bodies were divided into three long lobes, or segments, from head to tail. The name trilobite means "three-lobed."

Trilobites lived all over the world from the Cambrian to the end of the Permian Period, and there were many kinds. Some had extravagant spines that stuck out of the tops of their hard shells or from their sides. The tower-eyed trilobites, such as Erbenochile, were named for their extraordinarily tall eyes. Each of Erbenochile's eyes had more than 400 lenses and an overhanging piece of shell, which protected it like an eyebrow.

Erbenochile. Devonian Period, Africa. These fossils from Morocco are around 400 million years old and show Erbenochile's central spiny lobe, with the other two lobes on either side.

Archaeopteris

Have you ever seen a towering conifer tree, with cones and needlelike leaves? Or a feathery fern with long fronds? Combine the two and you get Archaeopteris (ar-kee-OP-ter-iss)! Its surprising mix of conifer and fern features meant that when its leaves and trunks were discovered, they were thought to belong to different species. In fact, Archaeopteris was a link between ferns and trees—it had a tall, woody trunk, but reproduced using tiny spores rather than seeds.

Archaeopteris was very successful and it formed forests around the world, growing in wet ground close to rivers. It is thought that its fallen leaves added nutrients to the soil as they rotted, making the soil richer.

Archaeopteris was one of the first
trees to grow on Earth.

**Archaeopteris. Devonian
to Carboniferous periods,
Worldwide.** This fossil shows
a fernlike frond of Archaeopteris.

Heliophyllum

Heliophyllum (he-lee-oh-FIE-lum) was a type of coral that today can be used as a fossil calendar! Its soft body, called a coral polyp, did not fossilize, but its hard, horn-shaped outer skeleton did. When the coral was alive, it added one layer to the top of its skeleton every day. By counting the number of layers in the fossil we can figure out that in the Devonian Period, when Heliophyllum lived, there were 420 days in a year—55 days more than the 365 we have now.

Heliophyllum lived alone, with the pointed end of its skeleton stuck into the sand of the seafloor. Just like a modern coral, it had tentacles that waved in the water to trap microscopic bits of food.

Heliophyllum. Devonian Period, Africa, North America, and South America. Heliophyllum fossils are shaped like a horn and have a cup at one end in which the coral polyp lived.

Heliophyllum was a type of rugose coral—rugose means "wrinkly."

Dunkleosteus

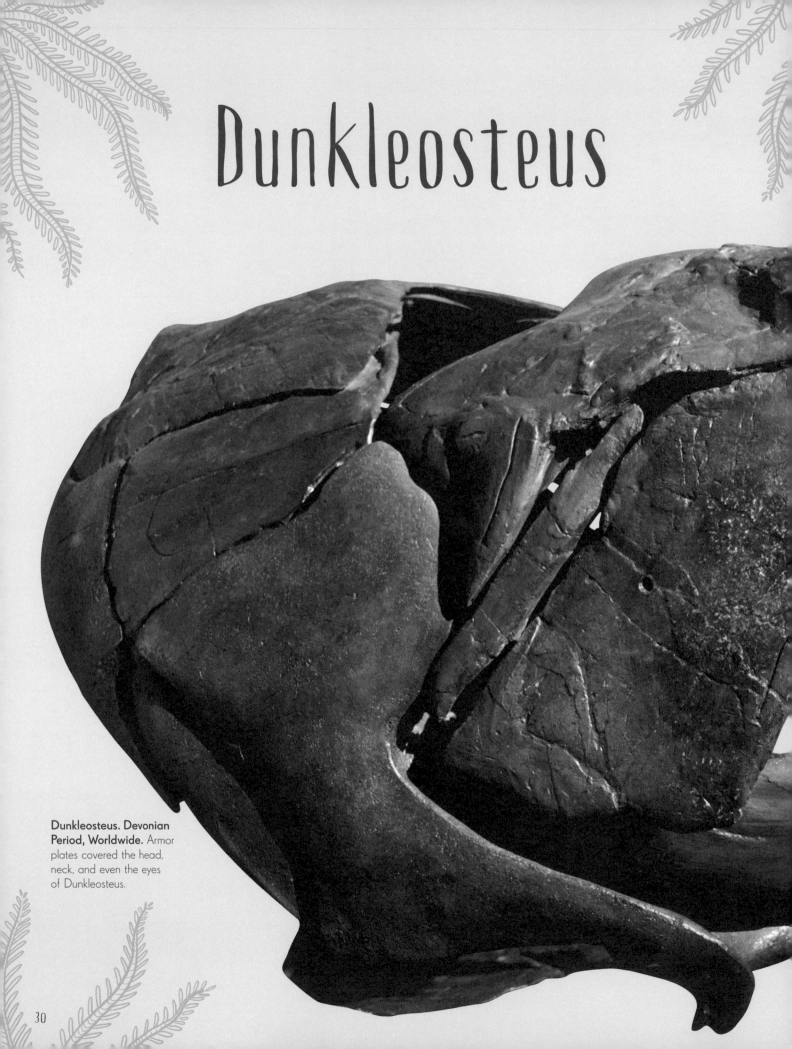

Dunkleosteus. Devonian Period, Worldwide. Armor plates covered the head, neck, and even the eyes of Dunkleosteus.

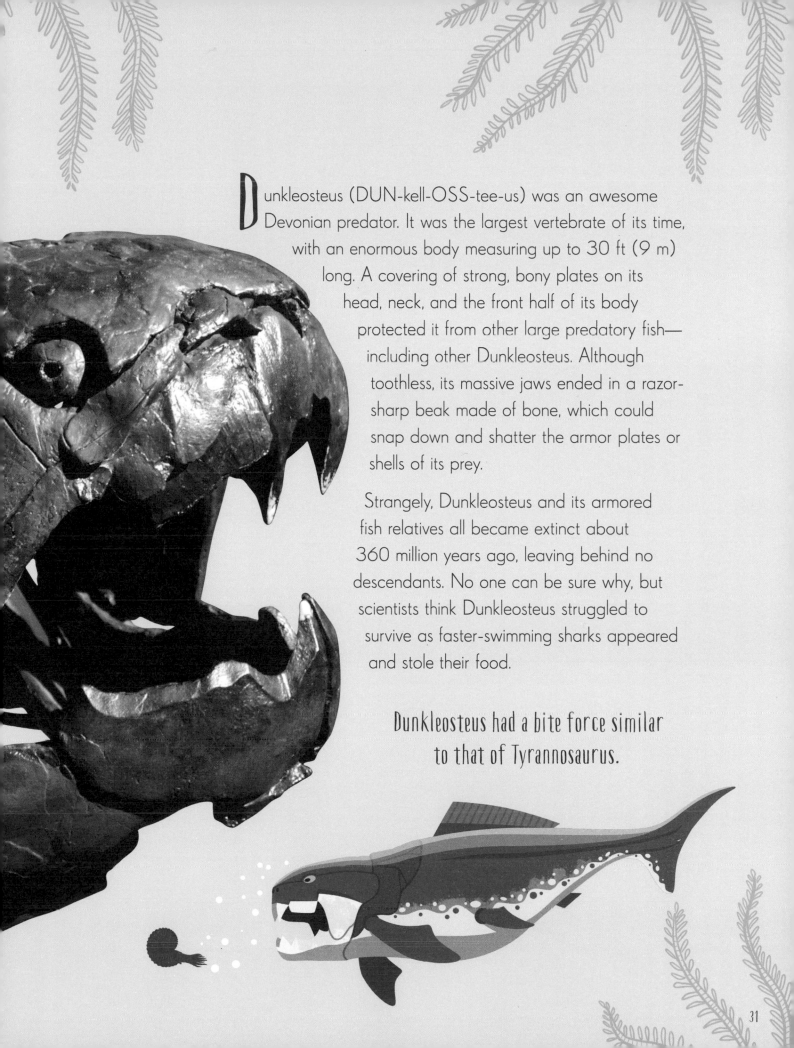

Dunkleosteus (DUN-kell-OSS-tee-us) was an awesome Devonian predator. It was the largest vertebrate of its time, with an enormous body measuring up to 30 ft (9 m) long. A covering of strong, bony plates on its head, neck, and the front half of its body protected it from other large predatory fish—including other Dunkleosteus. Although toothless, its massive jaws ended in a razor-sharp beak made of bone, which could snap down and shatter the armor plates or shells of its prey.

Strangely, Dunkleosteus and its armored fish relatives all became extinct about 360 million years ago, leaving behind no descendants. No one can be sure why, but scientists think Dunkleosteus struggled to survive as faster-swimming sharks appeared and stole their food.

Dunkleosteus had a bite force similar to that of Tyrannosaurus.

Tiktaalik

Imagine sitting by a pond and seeing a fish crawl out of the water and onto land! The amazing Tiktaalik (tik-TAA-lick) could do just that. It had a mix of fish and tetrapod, or four-legged animal, features. Like a fish, it had fins and scales, but other parts of its body, such as its flattened skull, strong limbs, and movable neck, were more like those of early amphibians. It had both lungs and gills, and scientists think that Tiktaalik could have clambered over muddy riverbanks, as well as swum in lakes.

The discovery of Tiktaalik's fossils was very important. Its "fishapod" characteristics show how land animals evolved from aquatic animals around 375 million years ago.

Tiktaalik. Devonian Period, North America. Tiktaalik had a triangular-shaped head and eyes that pointed upward.

Tiktaalik means "large, freshwater fish" in Inuktitut, the language of the people who live where its fossils were found in the Arctic.

Ichthyostega. Devonian Period, North America. Can you see the seven toes on Ichthyostega's paddlelike back foot?

Ichthyostega was one of the first
four-legged animals on Earth.

Ichthyostega

Much like Tiktaalik, Ichthyostega (ick-thee-oh-STAY-gah) was a bit
like a fish, but also a bit like an amphibian. It lived 370 million
years ago, around 5 million years after Tiktaalik, and it had both gills
to breathe underwater and lungs for breathing air. It could also swim,
as well as crawl on land. However, unlike Tiktaalik, Ichthyostega
had stout legs rather than fins, which could support its body as it
dragged itself between swampy ponds. Unusually, Ichthyostega had
seven toes on its back feet! These were probably webbed to help it
swim. Ichthyostega's eyes were on top of its head and it had good
eyesight for hunting. It snapped up its victims in its long, sharp teeth.

Moving onto land

Early life on Earth was only found in water. Algae floated in the ocean, and fish swam through rivers and seas. The move onto land posed many challenges for these aquatic organisms. How would they not dry out? And how would they walk? Plants developed a waxy coating, called a cuticle, to stop them from losing water, and they grew strong stems to keep them upright. Meanwhile, lobe-finned fish evolved slimy coatings or scales to stop themselves from drying out, and their fins transformed into limbs so they could crawl and run. These changes took many millions of years to happen though!

Charophyte
DNA studies show that plants are most closely related to green algae called charophytes (CAR-oh-fites). How and when plants moved onto land is hard to tell, but we know that they were there by around 473 million years ago.

Lepidodendron
One of the first really tall plants was treelike Lepidodendron (LEP-i-doh-DEN-dron). It could reach heights of 165 ft (50 m) because it had a strong trunk and an internal transportation system to move water and nutrients around.

Sciadophyton
Sciadophyton (SIGH-a-DOH-fite-on) was an early plant known from the Devonian Period. It developed an important feature for life on land—cup-shaped structures that stopped its reproductive cells from drying out.

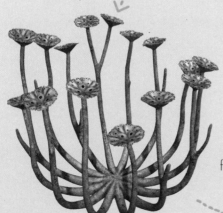

Eusthenopteron

Eusthenopteron (YOOS-then-OP-ter-on) is an example of a lobe-finned fish that lived in the Devonian Period. Lobe-finned fish had limblike fins and are thought to be the ancestors of tetrapods—animals with four legs.

Tiktaalik

Also called a "fishapod," Tiktaalik (tik-TAA-lick) had features that were a mix of both lobe-finned fish and early four-legged tetrapods. Even though it lived in water, it may have been able to crawl out onto land.

Ichthyostega

Ichthyostega (ICK-thee-oh-STAY-gah) is thought to have been an early tetrapod that lived in shallow swamps toward the end of the Devonian Period. It had lungs that allowed it to breathe air and four legs to support its body.

Eryops

Carnivorous Eryops (EH-ree-ops) was an amphibian that was able to live both on land and in water. However, it needed to lay its eggs in water—the development of hard-shelled eggs in reptiles allowed them to move farther onto land.

Aviculopecten

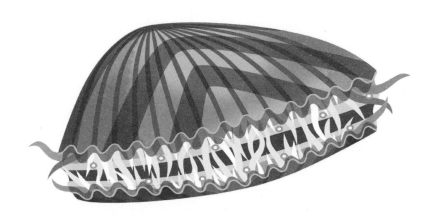

Aviculopecten (a-VIK-you-low-PECK-ten) was a bivalve—a type of soft-bodied animal that has two hard shells, or valves, of equal size. There are many bivalves alive today, including mussels, oysters, and scallops. Aviculopecten's shell was fan-shaped and had a zigzag pattern across it. It is possible that the dark lines helped hide the creature in its surroundings and stopped it from being spotted by predators. The hard case also protected Aviculopecten's soft insides, but it poked its tentacles out to catch tiny plankton to eat.

Bivalves first arrived around 541 million years ago during the Cambrian Explosion, a time when lots of new types of animals appeared. However, Aviculopecten lived much later, during the Devonian Period onward.

Aviculopecten. Devonian to Triassic periods, Worldwide.
The zigzag pattern on these Aviculopecten shells has survived for around 360 million years.

Only Aviculopecten's tough shells
survived the fossilization process
and are found as fossils.

Much of the coal used today comes from fossilized Lepidodendron forests that died more than 300 million years ago.

Lepidodendron

A young Lepidodendron (leppy-doe-DEN-dron) looked like a bottlebrush, with a spray of narrow leaves at the top of its trunk. As it grew, its lower leaves fell off, which left teardrop-shaped scars where they had once joined the trunk. The pattern of leaf scars on its fossils gives Lepidodendron its other name—"scale tree." This towering tree was one of the world's first large land plants. It could reach 165 ft (50 m) in height and grew unusual, rootlike branches at its base to help keep it upright.

Lepidodendron formed dense forests that absorbed huge amounts of carbon dioxide from the atmosphere. Carbon dioxide warms the Earth, and its loss may have led to the ice age at the end of the Carboniferous Period.

Lepidodendron. Carboniferous Period, Worldwide. Although they look like reptile scales, these are the scars left by old leaves falling off Lepidodendron's trunk.

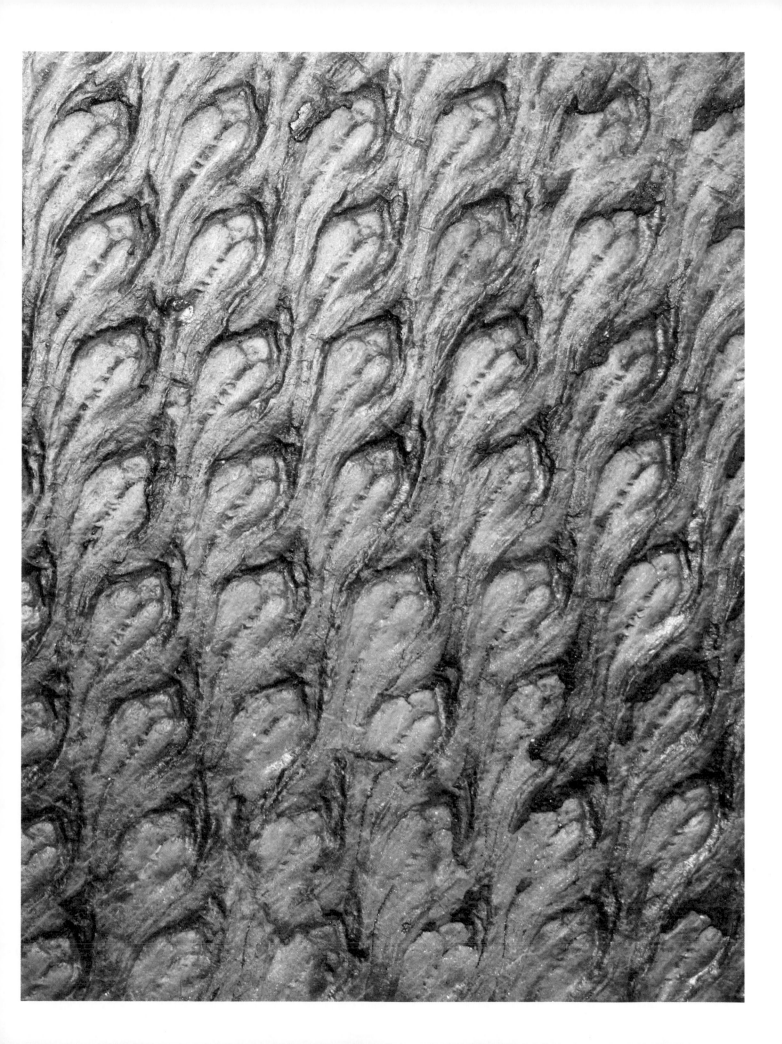

Calamites. Carboniferous Period, Worldwide. Fossils of Calamites' leaves are known as Annularia (ANN-nu-LAIR-ee-a), as they were discovered separately from its trunk.

Horsetails are referred to as "living fossils," because they existed a long time ago but are still found today.

Calamites

Modern horsetail plants grow low to the ground and are named after their resemblance to a hairy horse's tail. However, ancient horsetails, such as Calamites (CAL-a-MIGHT-eez), could be as tall as trees! They were among the first plants to have strong, upright stems and this enabled them to grow to huge heights. Calamites had a long, bamboolike trunk and it could be 165 ft (50 m) tall. Sprays of leaves grew from its branches, which may have been attractive to hungry herbivores.

Calamites lived more than 300 million years ago alongside Lepidodendron. It reproduced by releasing minute spores rather than seeds, which were produced in conelike structures called strobili at the tips of its branches.

Arthropleura

Arthropleura was the largest ever land-living
invertebrate (animal without a backbone).

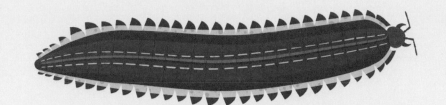

A distant relative of millipedes and centipedes, Arthropleura (arth-row-PLOO-ra) was one giant creepy-crawly. It could reach 8 ft (2.5 m) in length—that's longer than a cheetah! It is thought that Arthropleura was able to reach such big proportions because of the higher amounts of oxygen in the atmosphere when it was alive, around 300 million years ago. It lived in swampy forests searching for plants to chomp and was, in fact, one of the earliest large herbivorous land animals.

Arthropleura's body was divided into about 30 segments, all covered by tough plates. Fossilized Arthropleura footprints look a little like train tracks and show that it could grow up to 20 in (50 cm) wide.

Arthropleura.
Carboniferous Period,
Europe and North America.
This fossil shows part of one
of Arthropleura's jointed legs.

Griffinflies were the largest flying insects that have ever lived.

Meganeura

Can you imagine a flying insect the size of a falcon? Giant bugs were common in the skies 300 million years ago. Although it looked like a dragonfly, Meganeura (MEGA-new-ra) was actually a griffinfly, which was only distantly related. Flitting around on its enormous wings, Meganeura mostly preyed on other insects, but it was big enough to snatch up small lizards as well. Zooming down from above, it used special spines on its legs to grip prey, so once it had a hold there was no escape.

Why don't giant insects exist today? In the Carboniferous Period, there was much more oxygen in the atmosphere, which may have allowed insects to breathe more easily and grow much bigger.

Deltoblastus

Blastoids lived on Earth from around 472 million years ago
to around 252 million years ago, when they died out
in a mass extinction event.

Deltoblastus. Permian Period, Asia. Each one of these Deltoblastus theca, or body, fossils could easily fit in the palm of your hand.

Swaying gently underwater, with feathered fronds on top of a long stalk, this creature could easily be mistaken for a plant. However, it was actually a relative of sea stars and sea urchins, called a blastoid, or sea bud. Blastoids, such as Deltoblastus (DELL-toe-blas-tuss), lived in the ocean. They had stems anchoring them to the seafloor, with their bodies, called a theca (THEE-ka), at the top. The theca was protected by hard plates and had five grooves arranged in a star shape. Fine, hairlike tentacles stuck out from the grooves and trapped tiny food particles in the water. These were passed to the mouth hidden among the tentacles.

Dimetrodon

Dimetrodon could grow up to 15 ft (4.6 m) long—that's about the length of a saltwater crocodile.

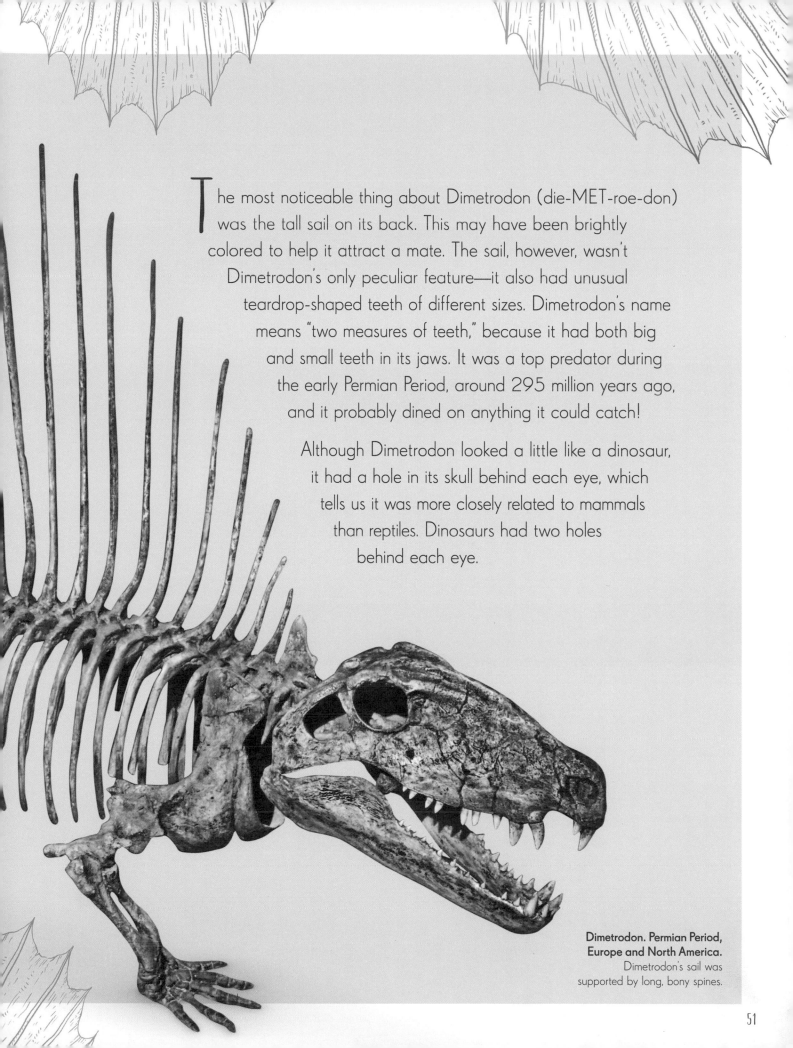

The most noticeable thing about Dimetrodon (die-MET-roe-don) was the tall sail on its back. This may have been brightly colored to help it attract a mate. The sail, however, wasn't Dimetrodon's only peculiar feature—it also had unusual teardrop-shaped teeth of different sizes. Dimetrodon's name means "two measures of teeth," because it had both big and small teeth in its jaws. It was a top predator during the early Permian Period, around 295 million years ago, and it probably dined on anything it could catch!

Although Dimetrodon looked a little like a dinosaur, it had a hole in its skull behind each eye, which tells us it was more closely related to mammals than reptiles. Dinosaurs had two holes behind each eye.

Dimetrodon. Permian Period, Europe and North America.
Dimetrodon's sail was supported by long, bony spines.

Seymouria's jaws were filled with pointed teeth—
it even had teeth in the roof of its mouth.

Seymouria

Just by looking at its skeleton, you may wonder what kind of animal Seymouria (see-MORE-ee-ah) was. It had a wide, triangular-shaped skull, which is typical of an amphibian, but also strong legs that could have held its body high off the ground, more like a reptile. In fact, 290-million-year-old Seymouria is thought to be a link between amphibians and early reptiles. It probably lived mainly on land, hunting for invertebrates and plants. Fossils of close relatives of Seymouria, however, suggest that its young may have had gills. This means that, like a frog, Seymouria underwent metamorphosis as it grew—transforming from a water-living larva to a land-living adult.

Seymouria. Permian Period, Europe and North America. Seymouria's strong legs and ribs suggest that it walked on land.

Helicoprion. Permian Period, Worldwide. This coiled Helicoprion tooth whorl shows the older, smaller teeth toward the middle of the spiral.

Helicoprion

Helicoprion (HELL-ee-coe-PRY-on) was a bizarre fish that looked a little like a shark with a circular saw in its mouth. Its skeleton was made of soft cartilage and so it is mainly known from fossils of its odd, coiled teeth, which are known as "tooth whorls." As the fish grew, bigger teeth formed on the outside of the whorl and the older, smaller teeth were pushed into the center of the spiral.

For more than 100 years, no one knew where the tooth whorl was positioned. Paleontologists placed it on Helicoprion's tail, nose, or even its back! New finds, however, show the tooth whorl made up the lower jaw. When Helicoprion closed its mouth, the teeth rotated backward, trapping and shredding its soft-bodied prey.

Although sharklike in appearance, 280-million-year-old Helicoprion was more closely related to modern ratfish, which are also called chimaeras.

Todites. Permian to Jurassic periods, Asia and Europe. This frond of Todites shows the leaflets branching off the main stalk.

Todites

Ferns have existed for around 360 million years, and they are still found around the globe today.

Most big herbivores in the Jurassic Period would have been happy to come across a leafy Todites (toe-DIE-teez). These ferns had a spray of green fronds that unfurled from their base. Todites was part of the royal fern family, and some of its relatives still exist today.

Fossils of Todites show the leaves that produced the tiny spores from which new ferns grew. The spores were found in clusters on the underside of the fronds. When the fern was not making spores, its leaves looked very different. In fact, fossils of the leaves without spores are given a completely different name—Cladophlebis (CLAD-oh-FLEB-iss)!

Mesozoic Era

252–66 Million Years Ago (MYA)

The Mesozoic Era is also known as the "Age of Reptiles." It is divided into three periods: the Triassic, Jurassic, and Cretaceous, and from the late Triassic dinosaurs appeared and eventually became the dominant land animals. An array of reptiles also ruled the seas and the skies. Dramatic changes in the land occurred during this era—the supercontinent, Pangea, split apart, and by the end of the Cretaceous the continents were positioned almost as they are today. This era ended with a bang when a giant asteroid hit the Earth, wiping out huge numbers of organisms.

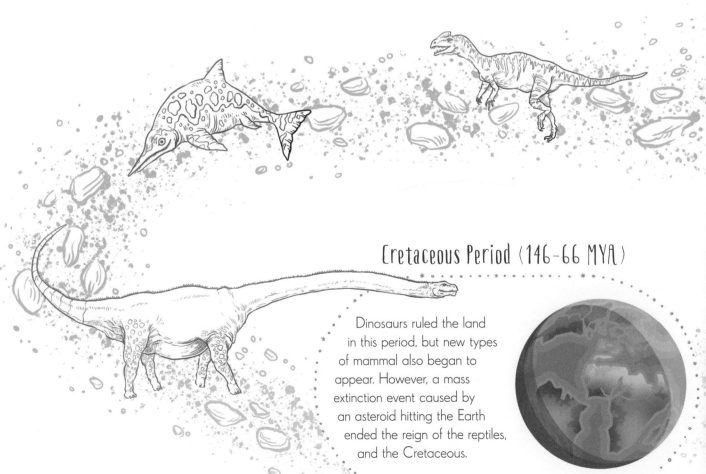

Cretaceous Period (146–66 MYA)

Dinosaurs ruled the land in this period, but new types of mammal also began to appear. However, a mass extinction event caused by an asteroid hitting the Earth ended the reign of the reptiles, and the Cretaceous.

Triassic Period (252–201 MYA)

During the Triassic, Pangea began breaking up and formed two new continents: Laurasia and Gondwana. Conifer forests spread across the land and both mammals and dinosaurs first appeared, but this period ended with a mass extinction event.

Jurassic Period (201–146 MYA)

Dinosaurs, crocodiles, and pterosaurs dominated the land in the Jurassic. By the middle of this period, the first birds evolved from dinosaurs and flowering plants began to bloom. The continents continued to split and drift apart.

Araucarioxylon

During the Triassic Period, giant conifer trees, such as Araucarioxylon (a-ROCK-air-EE-ox-i-lon), formed dense forests in Arizona. Today, their fossilized tree trunks are petrified, which means "turned to stone." Petrification can happen when a tree dies and is buried by volcanic ash. Over time, minerals from the ash, such as quartz, replace the wood. The petrified wood can be very colorful and is sometimes called "rainbow wood." The bright colors come from the different materials in the minerals; for example, red comes from iron and black comes from carbon. The wood is so well preserved that when a thin slice is examined under a microscope, the original cells of the plant can still be seen!

Petrified wood is so strong that it has been used as a building material.

Araucarioxylon. Triassic Period, North America. This Araucarioxylon trunk has been sliced across and polished to show the bright colors inside. You can still see the rings in the wood!

Herrerasaurus

Herrerasaurus fossils are found only in Argentina.

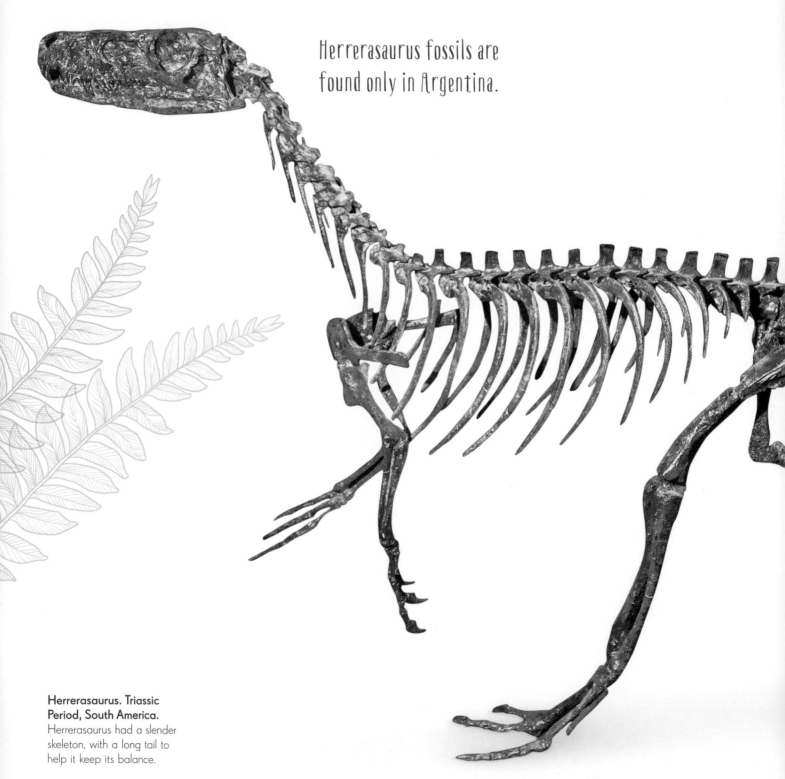

Herrerasaurus. Triassic Period, South America.
Herrerasaurus had a slender skeleton, with a long tail to help it keep its balance.

Herrerasaurus (heh-RARE-ra-SORE-uss) was one of the earliest dinosaurs. It lived around 230 million years ago in the Triassic Period, when dinosaurs first appeared. Scientists are still discussing what type of dinosaur it was, but it was definitely a meat-eater. Long, powerful legs made it a speedy sprinter, and its short arms were equipped with deadly, curved claws. Its jaws were lined with sharp teeth, which were perfect for gobbling up smaller herbivorous dinosaurs and other reptiles. Herrerasaurus's menacing weapons may also have been used for fighting each other—one fossil specimen shows puncture marks in its skull that may have been caused by the teeth of another Herrerasaurus.

Theropods

Most meat-eating dinosaurs belonged to the theropod (THERRO-pod) family. Many theropods had small arms, long legs, and sharp teeth and claws. They also usually walked on their back legs. However, they varied hugely in size and diet—smaller theropods ate invertebrates, such as insects; others ate fish; and the largest preyed on plant-eating dinosaurs. Some even ate plants! Although most dinosaurs died out during the mass extinction event at the end of the Cretaceous Period, some theropod dinosaurs survived—these survivors are birds.

Teeth Many theropods had sharp, pointed, and often serrated teeth for cutting up meat.

Spinosaurus

Spinosaurus (SPINE-oh-SORE-us) is the only dinosaur discovered that spent a large amount of time in water. It had a paddlelike tail that helped it swim as it hunted for fish in the rivers of Cretaceous Africa.

Claws Pointed claws were used to grip prey. Most theropods had three or four claws on their hands.

Cryolophosaurus

Cryolophosaurus (cry-o-LOAF-o-SORE-us) is known from fossils discovered in Antarctica. It had a crest on top of its head and may have been covered in fluffy feathers—as many theropods were.

Eodromaeus

This is one of the earliest dinosaurs—Eodromaeus (EE-oh-drom-ay-uss) appeared around 231 million years ago in the late Triassic Period. It was a lightweight hunter from South America.

Therizinosaurus

This unusual theropod was a herbivore. Therizinosaurus (THERRY-zin-oh-SORE-us) used its curved claws to defend itself, and it had a beak to help it browse on leaves.

Tail A long tail helped to balance a theropod's body weight as it walked on two legs.

Legs Theropods walked on their back legs and had feet with four toes—the fourth toe was smaller and found on the ankle.

Morganucodon

Morganucodon. Triassic to Jurassic periods, Asia and Europe.
This fossil shows the lower jaw of a Morganucodon and its sharp teeth.

Scurrying around, trying its best not to be seen, Morganucodon (MORE-gan-oo-CODE-on) was one of the earliest mammals to exist. It first appeared around 205 million years ago in Triassic forests. This small, furry creature was only the size of a mouse, but it had large eyes, which suggests that it was nocturnal. During the day, Morganucodon likely hid away in a burrow to avoid the snapping jaws of ravenous dinosaurs. At night, it scampered around the forest floor on a mission to find crunchy insects, which it could crush with its pointed teeth.

Unusually for a mammal, Morganucodon is thought to have laid small, leathery eggs—like platypuses and echidnas do today. However, it is likely that it fed its young with milk, as all mammals do.

Morganucodon had two sets of teeth during its life—the first set of baby teeth were replaced by permanent teeth as it grew.

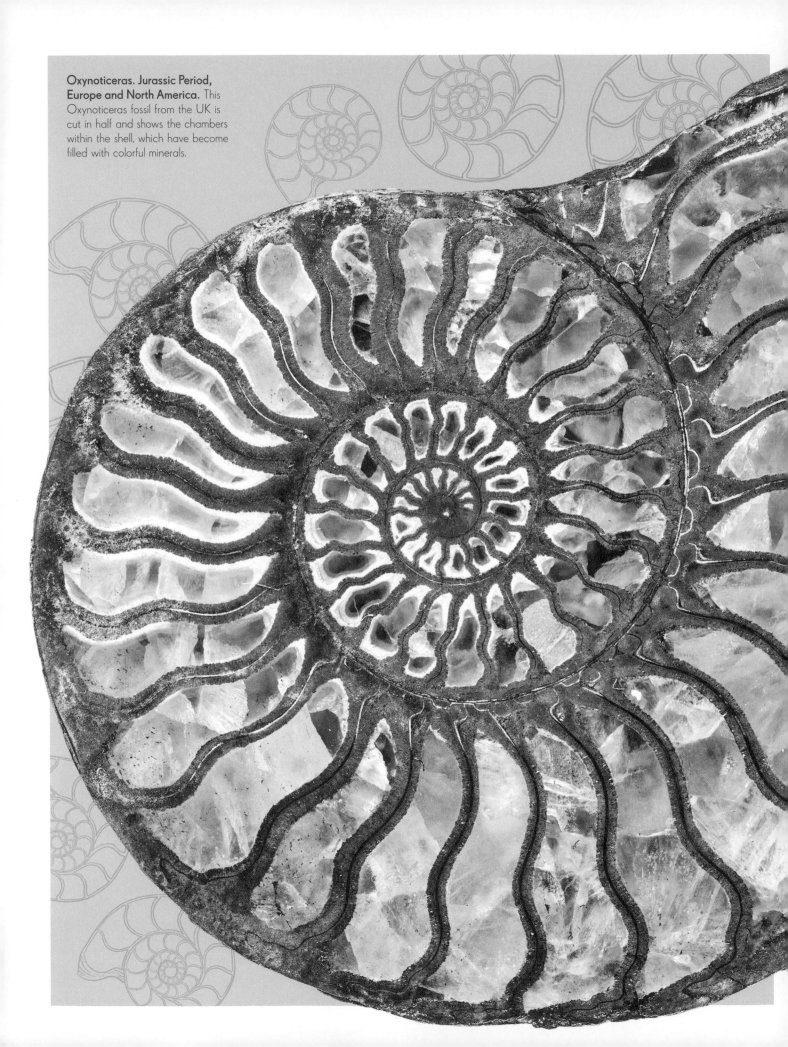

Oxynoticeras. Jurassic Period, Europe and North America. This Oxynoticeras fossil from the UK is cut in half and shows the chambers within the shell, which have become filled with colorful minerals.

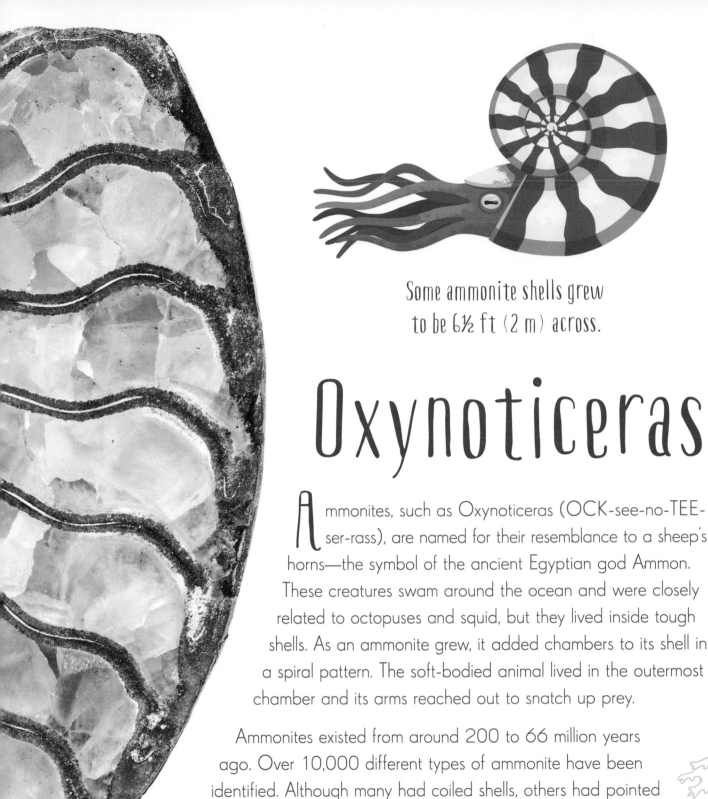

Some ammonite shells grew
to be 6½ ft (2 m) across.

Oxynoticeras

Ammonites, such as Oxynoticeras (OCK-see-no-TEE-ser-rass), are named for their resemblance to a sheep's horns—the symbol of the ancient Egyptian god Ammon. These creatures swam around the ocean and were closely related to octopuses and squid, but they lived inside tough shells. As an ammonite grew, it added chambers to its shell in a spiral pattern. The soft-bodied animal lived in the outermost chamber and its arms reached out to snatch up prey.

Ammonites existed from around 200 to 66 million years ago. Over 10,000 different types of ammonite have been identified. Although many had coiled shells, others had pointed shells, long shells that looked like trombones, or wiggly shells that looked like tangled balls of string!

Cryolophosaurus. Jurassic Period, Antarctica. This reconstructed fossil shows how Cryolophosaurus stood on two legs, using a long tail for balance.

Cryolophosaurus

Cryolophosaurus was the biggest meat-eating dinosaur on Earth when it was alive.

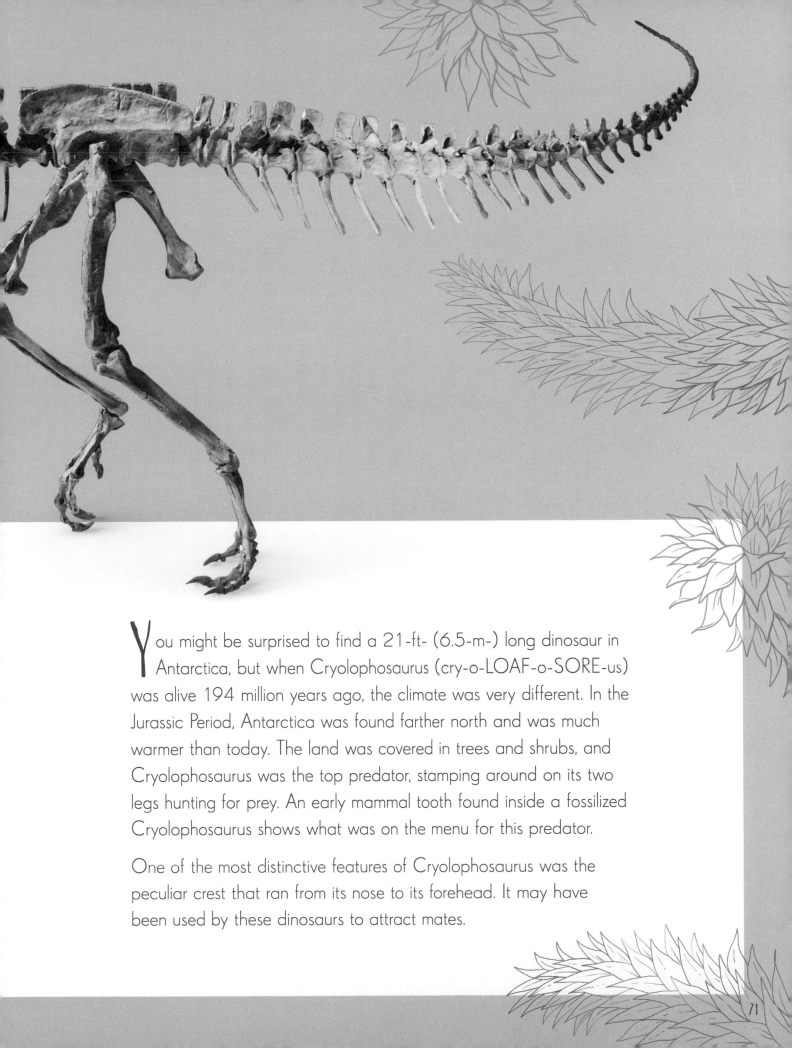

You might be surprised to find a 21-ft- (6.5-m-) long dinosaur in Antarctica, but when Cryolophosaurus (cry-o-LOAF-o-SORE-us) was alive 194 million years ago, the climate was very different. In the Jurassic Period, Antarctica was found farther north and was much warmer than today. The land was covered in trees and shrubs, and Cryolophosaurus was the top predator, stamping around on its two legs hunting for prey. An early mammal tooth found inside a fossilized Cryolophosaurus shows what was on the menu for this predator.

One of the most distinctive features of Cryolophosaurus was the peculiar crest that ran from its nose to its forehead. It may have been used by these dinosaurs to attract mates.

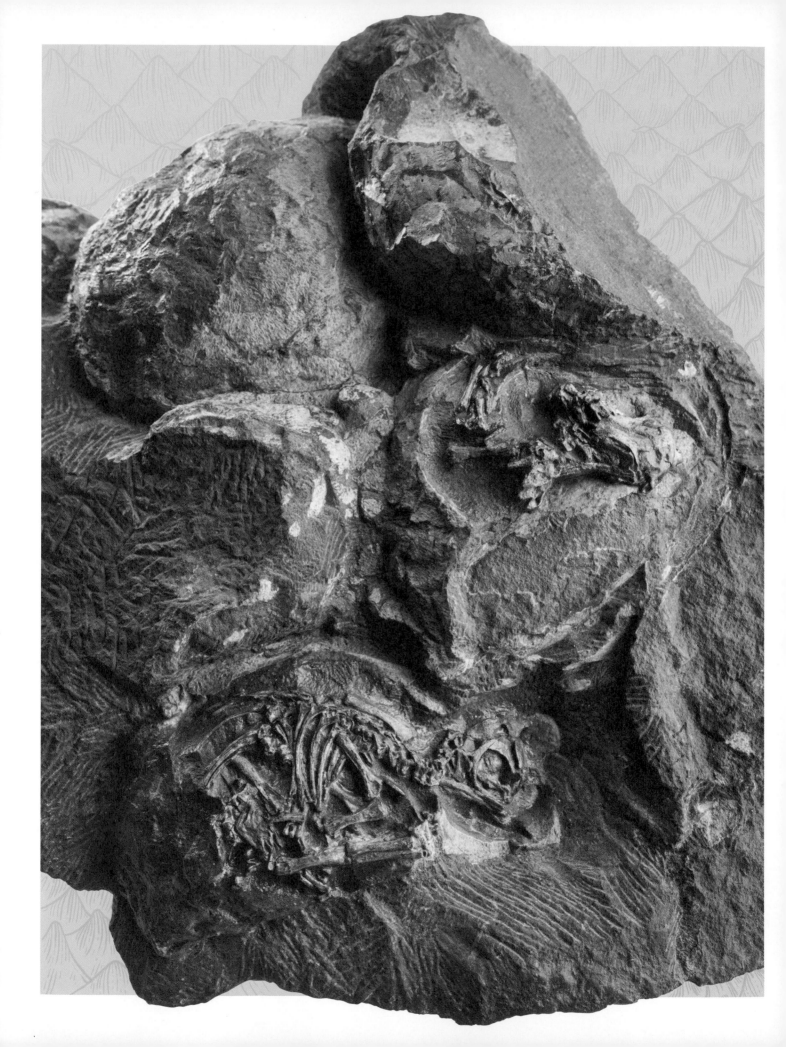

Massospondylus. Jurassic Period, Africa. These Massospondylus eggs were discovered in South Africa in 1976 and you can see the tiny dinosaurs inside them.

Massospondylus

Although Massospondylus (MASS-oh-SPON-dill-us) was not the first dinosaur to be discovered in Africa, in 1854 it became the first African dinosaur to be named. Massospondylus means "longer vertebrae" because of its long backbones. It was a fairly common dinosaur and it is known from many fossils. From studying its bones, scientists know that Massospondylus took more than 15 years to reach adult size—a huge 20 ft (6 m) from nose to tail.

Massospondylus laid oval-shaped eggs, about the size of duck eggs. In the 1970s, part of a 190-million-year-old Massospondylus nest was discovered that contained possibly the oldest dinosaur eggs ever found. Amazingly, tiny unhatched dinosaurs were preserved inside some of the eggs.

Baby Massospondylus walked on all fours,
but adults usually walked on two legs.

73

Stenopterygius. Jurassic Period, Europe. This well-preserved Stenopterygius fossil from Germany shows not just its fossilized bones and teeth, but also the outline of its body.

Stenopterygius

The word ichthyosaur comes from the ancient Greek and means "fish lizard."

With its torpedo-shaped body, powerful tail, and narrow flippers, Stenopterygius (sten-OP-terr-IDGE-ee-us) was able to whiz through the Jurassic seas. Its long, pointed snout was lined with lots of cone-shaped teeth, which it used to snap up its dinner. Its favorite foods were fish and squid.

Although it resembled a dolphin, Stenopterygius belonged to a group of marine reptiles known as ichthyosaurs. They existed from around 250 to 90 million years ago during the Mesozoic Era and ranged in size from about 3 ft (1 m) to 100 ft (30 m) long. Several ichthyosaur fossils have been found with babies inside them, which shows that they gave birth to live young. In fact, one Stenopterygius specimen was preserved while giving birth.

Lepidotes' body was covered in scales
that were hardened with enamel—
like our teeth.

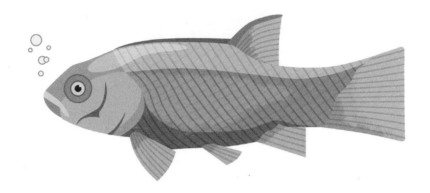

Lepidotes

Are they marbles? Or gemstones? No, they're the fossilized teeth of Lepidotes (leppy-DOE-tees). There were many species of this predatory fish, and they were common around 180 to 94 million years ago, during the Jurassic and Cretaceous periods. Lepidotes lived and hunted in both freshwater and shallow seas. Like modern carp, it could form its mouth into a tube and suck up shellfish and other invertebrates. Its hard, rounded teeth could then easily crush the tough shells.

When they were first discovered, Lepidotes' fossilized teeth were known as "toadstones." People believed that they grew inside toads and had magical powers that could protect against poison.

Lepidotes. Jurassic to Cretaceous periods, Worldwide. Lepidotes' teeth were round and clustered together.

Liopleurodon

Liopleurodon (LIE-oh-PLOOR-oh-don) was a type of marine reptile known as a pliosaur that thrived in the Jurassic Period. At 23 ft (7 m) long, it looked like a supersized crocodile with flippers. Liopleurodon was a top ocean predator. It was armed with vicious, spiked teeth that stuck out of its mouth, and it had flat, paddlelike limbs, which helped it power through the water. Its top snacks were probably smaller reptiles, squid, fish, or just about anything it wished! Unusually for a reptile, Liopleurodon gave birth to live young rather than laying eggs—it would have struggled to clamber onto land to build a nest.

Liopleurodon. Jurassic Period, Europe. Liopleurodon had incredibly long jaws, and four flippers to help it swim quickly.

A person's head is about one-eighth of their height, but Liopleurodon's head was about one-fifth of its total length.

Araucaria mirabilis

About 160 million years ago, a volcano erupted in Argentina and buried a forest of Araucaria mirabilis (ah-row-CARE-ee-a MIR-ah-BILL-iss) trees in ash. Over time, the trees became petrified, which means "turned to stone," and today the site is strewn with fossilized trunks and pine cones. Araucaria mirabilis was a conifer tree that was common in the Jurassic Period, and its cones were packed with seeds to produce new saplings.

Other species of Araucaria still survive, but they are found in far fewer places around the world than during the Mesozoic Era. Ancient Araucaria leaves were a favorite meal for long-necked sauropodomorph dinosaurs, which were one of the few herbivores that could reach them.

Araucaria mirabilis could grow to heights of 330 ft (100 m) — that's taller than a 30-story building!

Araucaria mirabilis. Jurassic Period, South America. This fossilized Araucaria cone has been cut in half and polished. The biggest cones were 3 in (8 cm) long.

Yi. Jurassic Period, Asia.
Yi is known from a single fossil discovered in China, in around 2007. Its feathers and teeth can be seen clearly.

Yi

Yi holds the record for the dinosaur with the shortest name.

Yi (yee) was an unusual dinosaur that looked like a cross between a bird and a bat! Like a bird, it had feathers covering most of its body and a pointed beak, but it also had batlike wings with flaps of skin stretched between its long fingers and wrists. Yi was the first bat-winged dinosaur to be discovered, but it was joined by Ambopteryx (am-BOP-ter-ix) in 2019.

About the size of a magpie, it is thought that Yi was a tree-dwelling dinosaur that used its wings to glide gently between branches. A few small teeth at the front of its jaw may have been used to snap up small animals in the forests where it lived around 159 million years ago.

Allosaurus

Allosaurus (AL-oh-SORE-us) looked a little like Tyrannosaurus, but although they both lived in North America, this dinosaur existed almost 100 million years before. While Allosaurus wasn't quite as large as Tyrannosaurus, it had bigger arms, each with three fingers ending in vicious, curved claws. Its teeth were long and jagged, and it was built to hunt. Studies of Allosaurus skulls suggest that it had an excellent sense of smell, which would have been very useful for sniffing out prey, such as Stegosaurus.

In addition to fossilized bones, some Allosaurus footprints have been identified. Fossil footprints are known as trace fossils, and they can tell us a lot about how dinosaurs moved. Allosaurus, for example, walked upright on two feet around 156 million years ago.

Allosaurus is known from many fossils of all ages,
from babies to teenagers and adults.

Allosaurus. Jurassic Period, North America.
This three-toed footprint is thought to have been made by a baby Allosaurus.

Stegosaurus

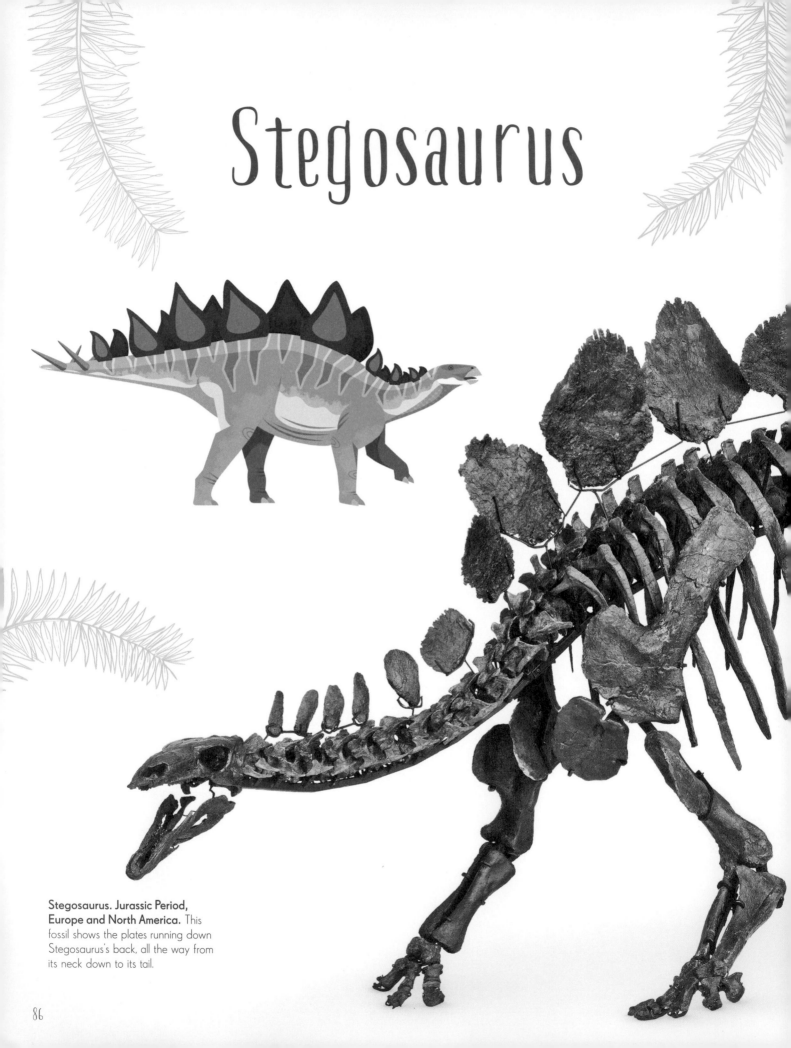

Stegosaurus. Jurassic Period, Europe and North America. This fossil shows the plates running down Stegosaurus's back, all the way from its neck down to its tail.

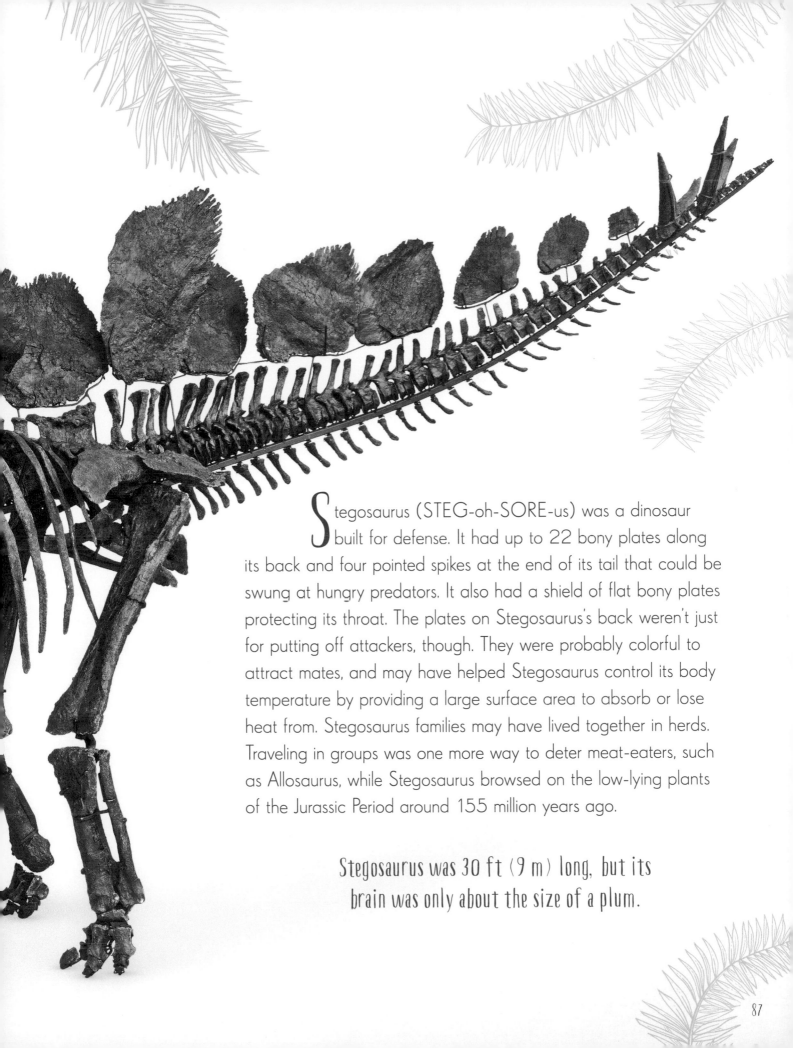

Stegosaurus (STEG-oh-SORE-us) was a dinosaur built for defense. It had up to 22 bony plates along its back and four pointed spikes at the end of its tail that could be swung at hungry predators. It also had a shield of flat bony plates protecting its throat. The plates on Stegosaurus's back weren't just for putting off attackers, though. They were probably colorful to attract mates, and may have helped Stegosaurus control its body temperature by providing a large surface area to absorb or lose heat from. Stegosaurus families may have lived together in herds. Traveling in groups was one more way to deter meat-eaters, such as Allosaurus, while Stegosaurus browsed on the low-lying plants of the Jurassic Period around 155 million years ago.

Stegosaurus was 30 ft (9 m) long, but its brain was only about the size of a plum.

Thyreophorans

Thyreophoran (THIGH-ree-OFF-oh-ran) means "shield bearer," and it's easy to see why the dinosaurs belonging to this group were given this name. Whether it was long tail spikes, pointed plates, or thick skin, these dinosaurs were covered in armor. Most thyreophorans were herbivores, and they were often preyed upon by meat-eaters. The thyreophorans can be split into two smaller groups: stegosaurs and ankylosaurs. Stegosaurs were recognizable from their large back plates and spike-covered tails. Ankylosaurs were more heavily built, with skin so thick and bony it was hard for a carnivore to bite through. Some even had macelike tail clubs to use as weapons.

Beak
Thyreophorans had sharp beaks to collect plants.

Plates Spiked plates acted as armor, but may have also been for showing off.

Tail spikes These spikes were dangerous weapons when swung from side to side.

Stegosaurus
Stegosaurus (STEG-oh-SORE-us) was a typical stegosaur. It had two rows of plates that ran along its back, and long spikes toward the tip of its tail. It even had a shield to protect its throat.

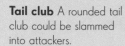

Tail club A rounded tail club could be slammed into attackers.

Armor Thick bony plates made ankylosaur skin extra strong.

Spikes Spikes and studs dotted the armor plating as extra protection.

Euoplocephalus

Ankylosaurs, such as Euoplocephalus (YOU-owe-plo-SEFF-ah-luss), were some of the most heavily armored dinosaurs to ever live. It had bone-reinforced skin, spikes, and a heavy tail club. Even large meat-eaters might have struggled to eat this Cretaceous herbivore.

Polacanthus

Not all ankylosaurs had tail clubs. Polacanthus (POLE-a-CAN-thuss) was a type of ankylosaur, known as a nodosaur, that didn't have weapons on their tails. It did, however, have lots of defensive spikes.

Kentrosaurus

Kentrosaurus (KEN-troh-SORE-us) was a spikier stegosaur than Stegosaurus. Its name means "spike lizard," because many of its back plates had become sharp and pointed. Like other stegosaurs, it had narrow jaws and browsed on leaves.

At 85 ft (26 m) long, Diplodocus was one
of the longest animals to ever live —
about as long as an average blue whale.

**Diplodocus. Jurassic
Period, North America.**
Diplodocus had a comb
of peglike teeth that it used
to strip leaves off branches.

Diplodocus

With its long neck and tail, Diplodocus (dip-LOD-oh-kus) was a typical sauropodomorph dinosaur. The whiplike tail contained about 80 bones, and Diplodocus may have swished it around for defense. The tail may also have helped balance the huge weight of Diplodocus's neck, so the dinosaur didn't fall over. It is not certain how high Diplodocus could hold its neck, but to reach tasty leaves on really high branches it may have reared up on its back legs, using its tail as a prop.

Impressions of dinosaur skin thought to be from Diplodocus have survived for more than 150 million years, since the dinosaur was alive. They suggest that Diplodocus had pencil-length spines along its neck, back, and tail.

Pterodactylus was the first flying reptile to be
discovered — it was found in Germany.

Pterodactylus

A member of the pterosaurs (TEH-roe-SORES)—a group
of flying reptiles that are often mistaken for dinosaurs—
Pterodactylus (TEH-roe-DACK-till-us) was a scaly, winged beast. It
soared through the skies 155 million years ago on batlike wings that
spanned up to 3 ft (1 m) across and stretched from the tip of its
long fourth finger all the way down to its legs.

Pterodactylus could fold up its wings and walk, which meant that
it was also a fierce predator on land. It had around 90 pointed
teeth, which it used to snap up invertebrates and other small animals.
Evidence suggests that, like many other pterosaurs, it had a crest
on its head, which may have been used to attract a mate.

Pterodactylus. Jurassic Period, Europe. Pterodactylus means "winged finger." This fossil shows the extra-long fourth finger, which supported the skin of its wing.

Kentrosaurus. Jurassic Period, Africa. This cast shows the space inside Kentrosaurus's spine that was thought—wrongly—to contain a second brain.

Kentrosaurus

Fossil evidence suggests that male and female Kentrosauruses had slightly different-shaped leg bones—but scientists don't know which one was which!

Like its North American relative Stegosaurus, Kentrosaurus (KEN-troh-SORE-us) also had rows of bony plates on its back. Instead of being broad and flat, however, this dinosaur's plates were more pointed, especially on its hips and tail. Its shoulder and tail spikes were particularly long and probably effective in keeping away predators. All Kentrosaurus fossils have been found in Tanzania in Jurassic rocks around 152 million years old. This means Kentrosaurus existed at the same time as Stegosaurus, but it was about half the size.

A large space in the fossil backbones of stegosaurs, such as Stegosaurus and Kentrosaurus, was found to be larger than the space left by their brain. This led to the wrong idea that stegosaurs had two brains!

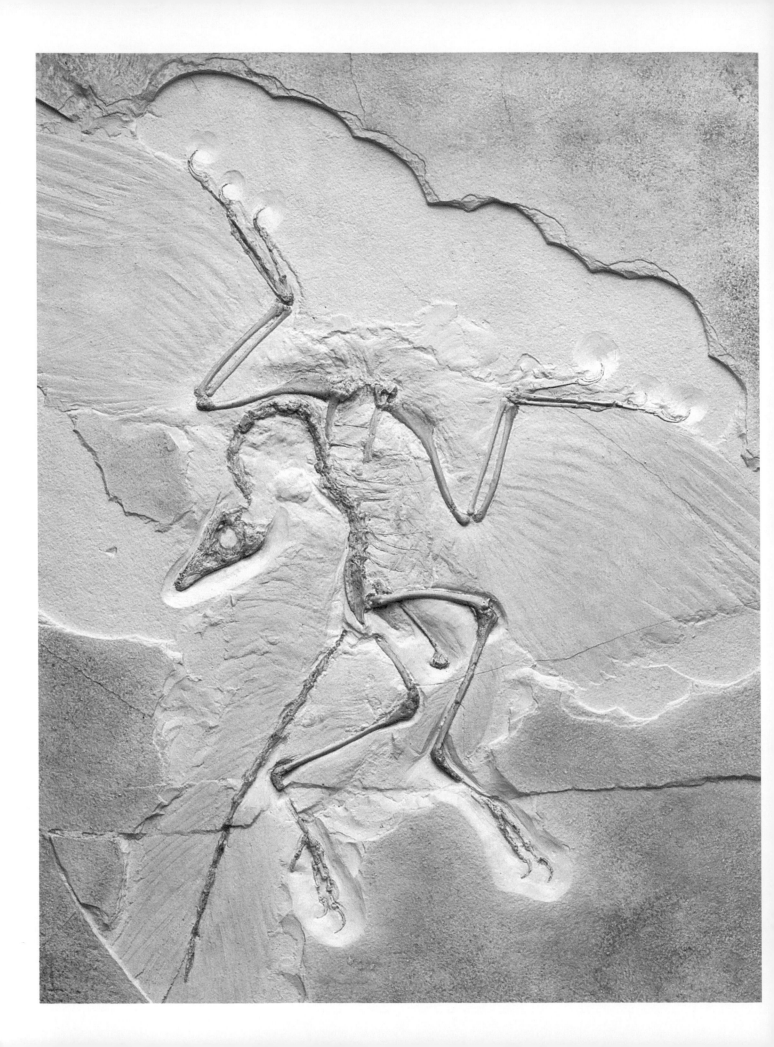

Archaeopteryx. Jurassic Period, Europe. The impressions of feathers can be seen on this fossil, known as the Berlin specimen, which was discovered in around 1870.

We know Archaeopteryx had a mix of dark and light feathers.

Archaeopteryx

Archaeopteryx (ar-kee-OP-ter-ix) was the first dinosaur with feathers to be discovered. Its fossils are special because they show it had a mixture of theropod dinosaur and bird features. For example, it had a long, bony tail and teeth, but also feathers and wings. This blend of characteristics in Archaeopteryx gave the first hint that birds and dinosaurs were closely related. Today, it is accepted that birds are dinosaurs, and that dinosaurs live on today as birds!

Archaeopteryx was about the size of a crow, but it could probably only flap its wings to fly or glide for short distances. It lived 150 million years ago, and spent its time hunting for small reptiles and insects to eat.

Sarcosuchus

Sarcosuchus. Cretaceous Period, Africa and South America. Sarcosuchus had a large, bony bump at the tip of its snout, but no one is sure what it was for.

Sarcosuchus's teeth were constantly replaced, which meant it had teeth of different sizes in its jaws.

About the length—and weight—of two cars, Sarcosuchus (sar-coe-SOO-kuss) was one of the largest crocodile-like animals that ever existed. Its skull alone was almost as long as an adult human, and its mouth was packed with more than 100 teeth. Sarcosuchus's wide snout suggests that it ate large land animals, including dinosaurs! As an ambush predator, it would have waited quietly below the surface of the water until an unsuspecting creature arrived for a drink and then... whoosh! Sarcosuchus would grab its dinner in one snap of its jaws.

Sarcosuchus appeared more than 130 million years ago and lived in freshwater habitats. Like modern crocodiles, it had bony bumps all over its back that helped protect it from attackers.

Polacanthus was covered with at least four different types of armor.

Polacanthus

Predators thought twice before attacking Polacanthus (POLE-a-CAN-thus). This 130-million-year-old dinosaur was heavily armored—its name means "many thorns," which refers to the fact that its body was covered in spikes and bony studs. The rows of spikes on its neck and sides were long and sharp, to put off any hungry meat-eating dinosaurs from trying to take a bite. Unusually for an ankylosaur dinosaur, prickly Polacanthus had a large, solid shield of bone on its back above its hips. This shield was dotted with extra bony bumps and would have been difficult for predators to pierce. With so much armor, this dinosaur weighed in at around 2.2 tons (2 metric tons)—heavier than a hippopotamus!

Polacanthus. Cretaceous Period, Europe. This fossilized Polacanthus skin shows the bony studs that protected it.

Iguanodon

In 1825, Iguanodon became the second dinosaur ever to be named — the first was Megalosaurus.

When Iguanodon (ig-GWAH-no-don) was first discovered, scientists weren't sure where to place the bony spike found with its skeleton. At first they thought it was a nose horn, but when more complete skeletons were found, they realized it was actually a thumb spike. The first fossils of Iguanodon identified were of its teeth, which resembled those of an iguana—in fact, Iguanodon means "iguana tooth."

Iguanodon lived more than 125 million years ago and plodded along on four legs, but it could also walk and run on two legs. It may have used its hands to bring branches close to its beak, which was ideal for snipping up plants. Its thumb spike might have been used to open fruits, or to defend itself from predators.

Iguanodon. Cretaceous Period, Europe. This fossil of the bones of Iguanodon's hand shows the thumb spike on the right.

Ornithopods

The best way to tell if a dinosaur belongs to the ornithopod (OR-nith-oh-pod) group is to see whether it has a beak for gathering plants, but no armor or weapons, like the thyreophorans and marginocephalians had. There were many types of ornithopod, but all were herbivores and most walked on two legs—although some could walk on all fours, too. One group of ornithopods were known as hadrosaurs, or "duck-billed dinosaurs," and many of them had unusual crests on their heads. These crests may have helped hadrosaurs to make loud noises or have been brightly colored to attract mates.

Tail A sturdy tail could be used as a prop when ornithopods reared up to reach leaves to eat.

Iguanodon
Iguanodon (ig-GWAH-no-don) lived in Cretaceous Europe. Like many ornithopods, it walked on either two or four feet, and used its arms to bring branches closer to its mouth.

Parasaurolophus

Parasaurolophus (PA-ra-SORE-oh-LOAF-us) was a hadrosaur, and it had a long crest on its head. The crest may have helped this dinosaur to make loud sounds to communicate with other Parasaurolophus.

Edmontosaurus

This hadrosaur lived in North America in the Cretaceous Period. Edmontosaurus (ed-MONT-oh-SORE-us) used its wide, ducklike bill to harvest plants. At 40 ft (12 m) long, it could reach leaves from the ground right up to tree branches.

Beak A tough beak was used to cut leaves off shrubs and trees.

Teeth Ornithopods had teeth that were constantly replaced as they were worn down.

Maiasaura

Fossils of Maiasaura (MY-a-SORE-a) show that, like many ornithopods, it lived in herds. This dinosaur even nested in large groups, probably to help protect it from large predators.

Legs Many ornithopods had shorter front legs and longer back legs.

Psittacosaurus. Cretaceous Period, Asia. About 120 million years old, this fossil from China shows a complete Psittacosaurus skeleton.

Psittacosaurus

Psittacosaurus (si-tak-a-SORE-us) means "parrot lizard," and when you look at this dinosaur's beak you can see why. Its distinctive curved bill could be used like a pair of scissors to snip off leaves to eat, and its sharp-edged teeth shred them into pieces. Stones found in Psittacosaurus's stomach were probably gastroliths, which mashed up any extra tough plants and helped digestion.

This dinosaur was covered in scales, but the top of Psittacosaurus's tail had an unusual brush of quills, perhaps for showing off to mates. Scientists studying remains of Psittacosaurus's skin have discovered that it was darker on top and lighter underneath, which may have helped it to hide in its forest home.

Although Psittacosaurus only had two small cheek horns, and no frill, it was a ceratopsian and closely related to dinosaurs such as Triceratops.

Confuciusornis

At first glance, you might think Confuciusornis (con-FEW-shus-OR-niss) was like any other bird, but this 125-million-year-old animal still had some features of its dinosaur ancestors. Although it was covered in feathers and had large wings, Confuciusornis also had curved claws on its fingers, which might have helped it to climb among branches. The shape of its skeleton suggests Confuciusornis could fly, but it is not certain how far it could travel.

Some Confuciusornis fossils have long tail feathers, and it is thought these are males. One fossil without long tail feathers was found to contain a special type of bone only found in female birds before they lay eggs. This suggests that male and female Confuciusornis looked different, like many male and female birds today.

Confuciusornis was the first bird discovered with a toothless beak.

Confuciusornis. Cretaceous Period, Asia. This fossil shows the outline of Confuciusornis's feathers. The lack of long tail feathers suggests this is a female.

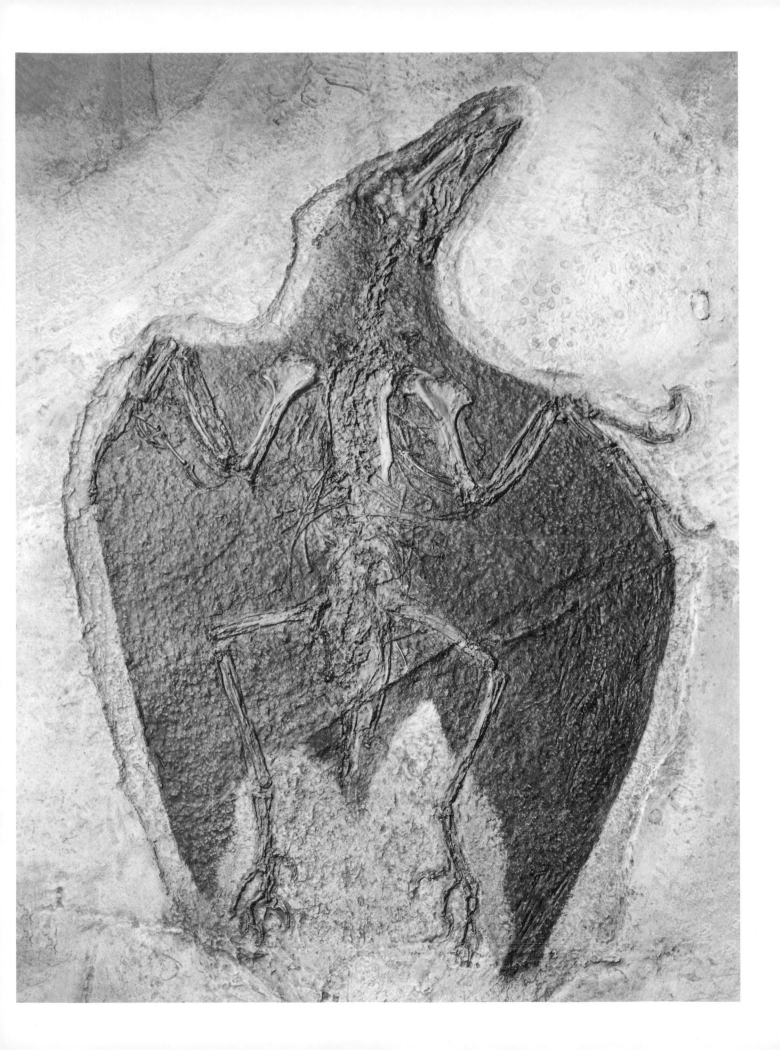

Sinosauropteryx

We know one of the Sinosauropteryx fossils discovered was female because unlaid eggs were found inside it!

All you might have seen of Sinosauropteryx (SIGH-no-sore-OP-ter-ix) was a flash of orange and white through the undergrowth. This small, meat-eating dinosaur lived 120 million years ago in the forests of Cretaceous Asia, chasing after small animals, such as lizards, to eat. Sinosauropteryx's fossils are beautifully preserved, and you can still see the outlines of the simple fuzzy feathers that covered its body. In fact, Sinosauropteryx was the first dinosaur without wings discovered to have feathers. Special pigment-filled structures found inside the feathers tell scientists all about its color. The top of Sinosauropteryx's body was reddish-orange, while its belly was lighter, and its tail was striped.

Sinosauropteryx. Cretaceous Period, Asia. This fossil of Sinosauropteryx from China shows the fuzzy feathers on its back and tail.

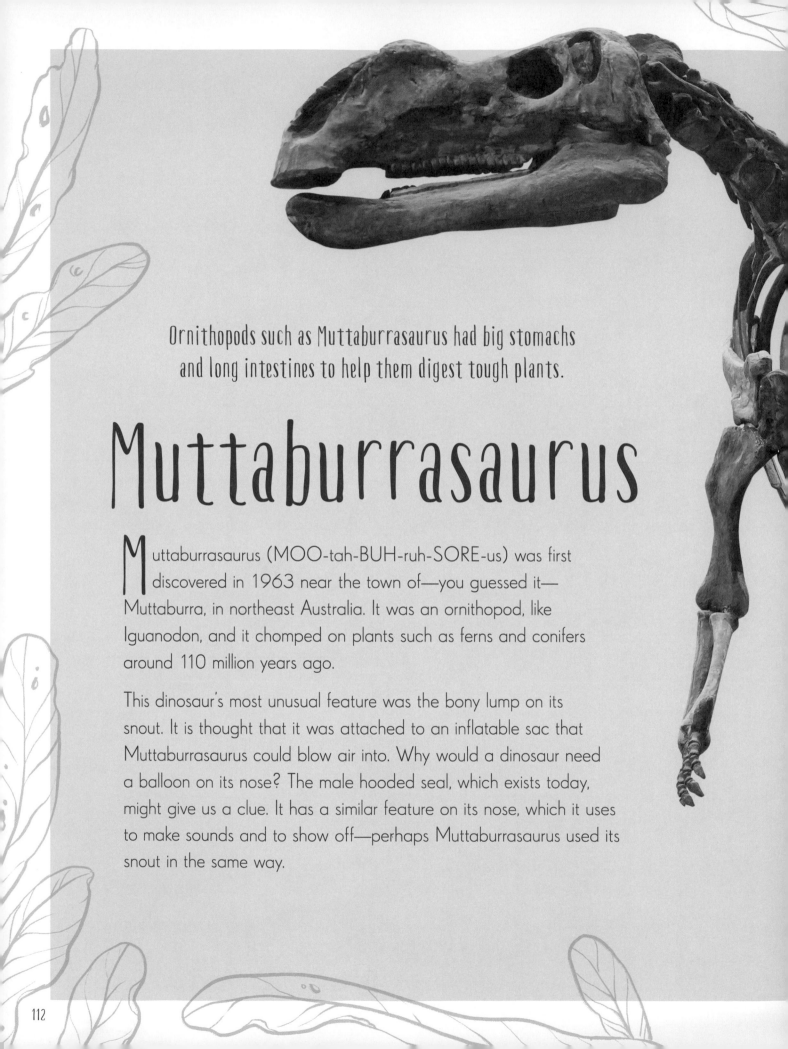

Ornithopods such as Muttaburrasaurus had big stomachs and long intestines to help them digest tough plants.

Muttaburrasaurus

Muttaburrasaurus (MOO-tah-BUH-ruh-SORE-us) was first discovered in 1963 near the town of—you guessed it—Muttaburra, in northeast Australia. It was an ornithopod, like Iguanodon, and it chomped on plants such as ferns and conifers around 110 million years ago.

This dinosaur's most unusual feature was the bony lump on its snout. It is thought that it was attached to an inflatable sac that Muttaburrasaurus could blow air into. Why would a dinosaur need a balloon on its nose? The male hooded seal, which exists today, might give us a clue. It has a similar feature on its nose, which it uses to make sounds and to show off—perhaps Muttaburrasaurus used its snout in the same way.

Muttaburrasaurus.
Cretaceous Period, Oceania.
Muttaburrasaurus could walk on
either two or four legs.

Belemnites could squirt out clouds of ink, like modern squid, and the fossilized ink can be used today as paint!

Neohibolites

The bullet-shaped fossils of belemnites (BELL-em-nights) are common. However, not all are as beautiful as this Neohibolites (NEE-oh-HIB-oh-lights) fossil. Belemnites were squishy, squidlike animals, but they were unusual in having a cone-shaped internal skeleton. These skeletons—also called guards—are often all that survive of these squashy creatures. Sometimes during fossilization, a mineral called silica replaced the hard skeleton and turned it into shiny blue and green opal, but most are gray and rocky. Some people believed that the fossils were thrown to the ground in thunderstorms, so they are also known as "thunderstones." Belemnites thrived in the Jurassic Period, when the ocean was much warmer. They zoomed around hunting for small fish to eat.

Neohibolites. Cretaceous Period, Worldwide. This colorful opal belemnite was found in Australia and shows the animal's pointed skeleton, or guard.

Patagotitan

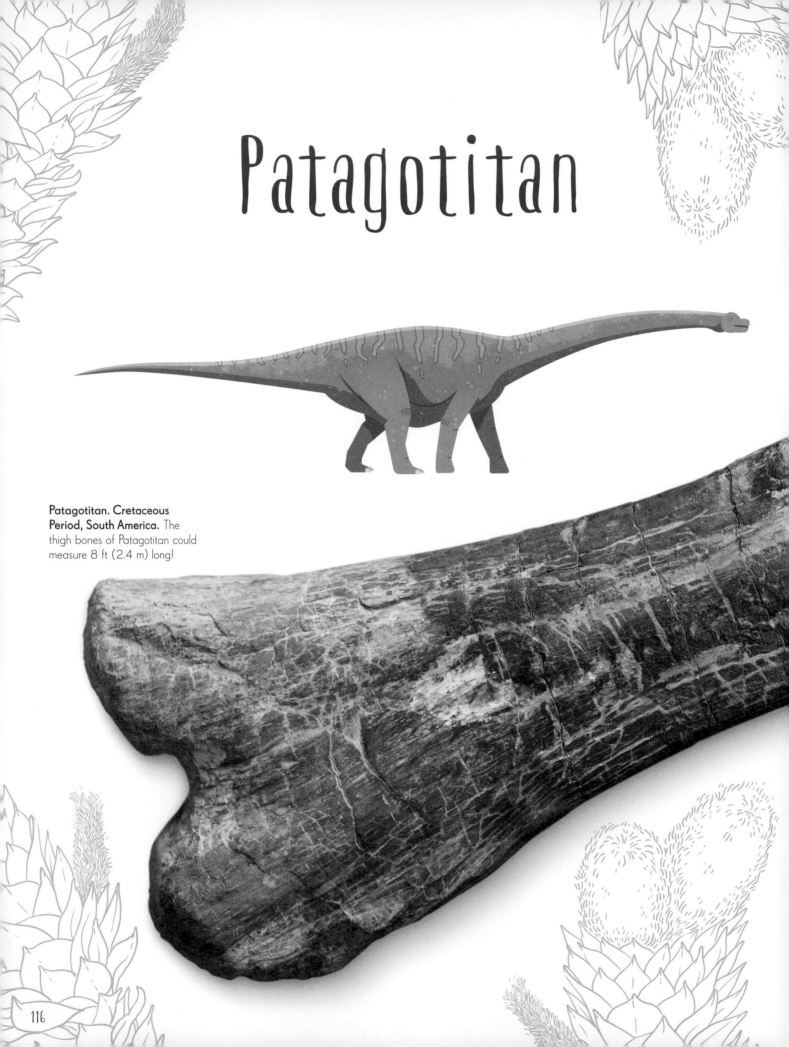

Patagotitan. Cretaceous Period, South America. The thigh bones of Patagotitan could measure 8 ft (2.4 m) long!

Patagotitan was one of the largest dinosaurs to ever exist.

Patagotitan (pat-AG-oh-tie-tan) was one mighty sauropodomorph. Around two and a half times longer than Tyrannosaurus, this dinosaur belonged to a group known as titanosaurs, meaning "titanic lizards." In recent years, several massive dinosaurs have been discovered, but because only pieces of them have been found, no one is certain which was the biggest. Patagotitan's long neck would have allowed it to reach the tops of tall conifer trees to browse on their leaves—and weighing in at up to 77 tons (70 metric tons), it needed to eat a lot! Despite their giant proportions, it is thought that titanosaur eggs were only about the size of ostrich eggs, so the baby dinosaurs had a lot of growing to do to reach their adult size.

Head Sauropodomorphs had small heads with peglike teeth for raking leaves off branches.

Diplodocus

A well-known sauropodomorph, Diplodocus (dip-LOD-oh-kus) had a very long neck and tail. It walked on four legs, which were incredibly strong and muscular to support its weight.

Long neck A long neck was used to reach leaves in trees that no other plant-eater could.

Claws Diplodocus had claws on all four feet, unlike the titanosaurs, which had claws only on their back legs.

Sauropodomorphs

With long necks and tails, the sauropodomorphs (SORE-oh-POD-oh-morfs) might be the easiest group of dinosaurs to spot. These humongous herbivores included the biggest dinosaurs to exist. Early sauropodomorphs didn't reach giant sizes and could walk on two legs, but, over the course of the Mesozoic Era, they grew bigger and bigger. By the Cretaceous Period, a group of sauropodomorphs called titanosaurs had appeared and they were colossal—species such as Argentinosaurus may have reached 110 tons (100 metric tons) in weight. These dinosaurs lived across the world, but became extinct with the other large dinosaurs at the end of the Cretaceous.

Argentinosaurus

Argentinosaurus (ARE-jen-TEEN-oh-SORE-us) was a titanosaur and may have been the biggest dinosaur to ever live. Scientists estimate it may have reached 115 ft (35 m) long! It lived in the Cretaceous Period in South America.

Long tail A long tail could be used like a whip against predators.

Massospondylus

An early sauropodomorph that lived in Jurassic Africa, Massospondylus (MASS-oh-SPON-dill-us) only grew to 20 ft (6 m) long. Even though it wasn't as big as other dinosaurs in this group, it still had a long neck and tail.

Giraffatitan

Unlike other sauropodomorphs, Giraffatitan (ji-RAF-a-TIE-tan) had a more upright neck, which allowed it to reach high into trees. It lived in Africa in the Jurassic Period and could reach 40 ft (12 m) tall.

Magnolia

Plants in the magnolia (mag-NOH-lee-a) family were among the first on Earth to produce flowers. Magnolias are still around today, but their earliest relatives lived around 100 million years ago, before the non-bird dinosaurs became extinct! The flowers of early magnolias formed big bowl shapes with large petals, known as tepals. At their center, they had a cluster of pollen-producing stamens that attracted pollen-eating beetles. Magnolia flowers had to be tough enough not to be damaged by the hungry beetles, but these insects did the important job of pollinating the flowers, so the plant could make seeds.

Unlike the soft blooms, the smooth-edged leaves of magnolias are often found as fossils. They look amazingly similar to the leaves of modern magnolias.

DNA has been successfully removed from a fossil magnolia leaf around 20 million years old!

Magnolia. Cretaceous Period to present, Worldwide. This magnolia leaf from the Cretaceous still clearly shows its central stem and pointed end.

Spinosaurus

Spinosaurus hunted for prey on land
and in the water.

Spinosaurus. Cretaceous Period, Africa. The smooth, conical shape of a Spinosaurus tooth was perfect for piercing rather than cutting.

You'd have to be careful going for a swim during the Cretaceous Period. Spinosaurus (SPINE-oh-SORE-us) was a terrifying predator that lived in Africa almost 100 million years ago, and it could hunt in water. It was the biggest meat-eating dinosaur to exist—longer even than a Tyrannosaurus—and it had strong arms and a paddlelike tail that might have helped push it through rivers. A long snout filled with pointed teeth and large, curved claws were perfect for catching prey, which were most likely large fish.

A tall sail along its spine made Spinosaurus look even more enormous. This might have helped it control its body temperature, or been brightly colored to show off to other Spinosaurus.

Hesperornis. Cretaceous Period, North America. A streamlined skeleton suggests that Hesperornis was an excellent diver.

Hesperornis

Hesperornis (HESS-per-ORE-niss) was an ancient large seabird that lived around 84 million years ago. It had tiny wings and could not fly, but instead spent most of its life bobbing on the surface of the ocean. Pushing itself along with its powerful back legs and webbed feet, Hesperornis dived underwater to snap up fish in its tooth-lined beak. As with all birds, Hesperornis nested on land, but its body—so graceful in water—was poorly adapted for walking, and it would not have traveled far from the coast.

Studies of Hesperornis's bones show that it could grow rapidly, reaching adult size within a single year! Bite marks on its fossils suggest that it was a target of marine reptiles.

Hesperornis fossils look very similar to the skeletons of grebes—modern diving birds.

Elasmosaurus

Elasmosaurus's neck was more than half of its body length!

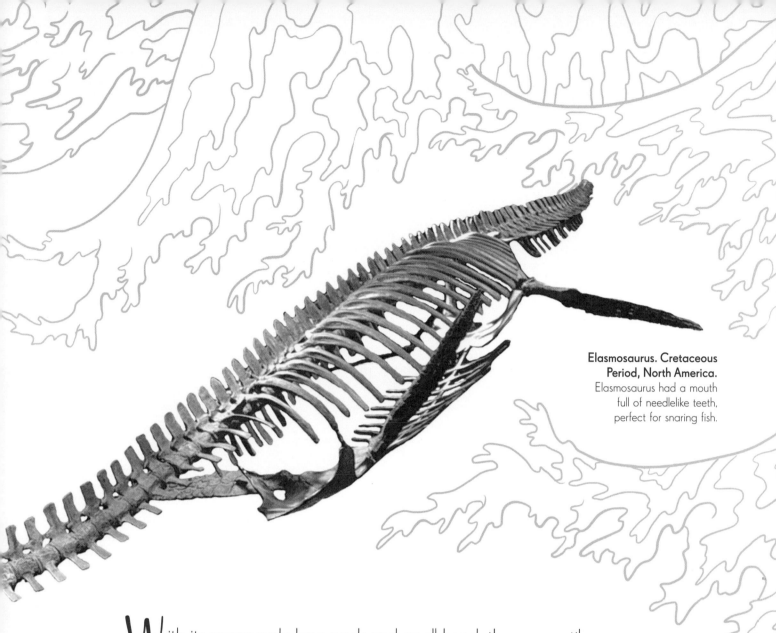

**Elasmosaurus. Cretaceous
Period, North America.**
Elasmosaurus had a mouth
full of needlelike teeth,
perfect for snaring fish.

With its enormously long neck and small head, the sea reptile
Elasmosaurus (el-LAZZ-moe-SORE-us) was nothing like any
animal alive today. Its neck contained around 70 bones, whereas its
tail had just 18. When it was first reconstructed, Elasmosaurus's head
was accidentally placed on its tail! Scientists aren't certain how much
Elasmosaurus could move its giant neck, but it may have used it to
pick up prey from the seafloor or to lunge at schools of fish.

Elasmosaurus lived around 80 million years ago and swam with four
paddlelike limbs. Like other plesiosaurs, it gave birth to live young, as
it would have struggled to get itself onto land to lay its eggs.

Maiasaura

Maiasaura means "good mother lizard," because it looked after its young.

More than 1,000 Maiasaura (MY-a-SORE-a) fossils have been discovered, of all ages, so we have a good understanding of how it grew and raised families. Maiasaura existed around 77 million years ago, living and nesting together in large herds where there were lots of watchful eyes to spot predators. Each Maiasaura mother carefully built a volcano-shaped nest of mud, in which it laid 30–40 eggs. The nests were spaced around 23 ft (7 m) apart, so it must have been tricky for the 30-ft- (9-m-) dinosaur to walk between them! Newly hatched Maiasaura were helpless and they relied on their parents to feed them vegetation, but they grew quickly. In just a year, a hatchling became the size of a sheep.

Maiasaura. Cretaceous Period, North America.
Maiasaura hatchlings had larger eyes and a shorter snout compared with an adult.

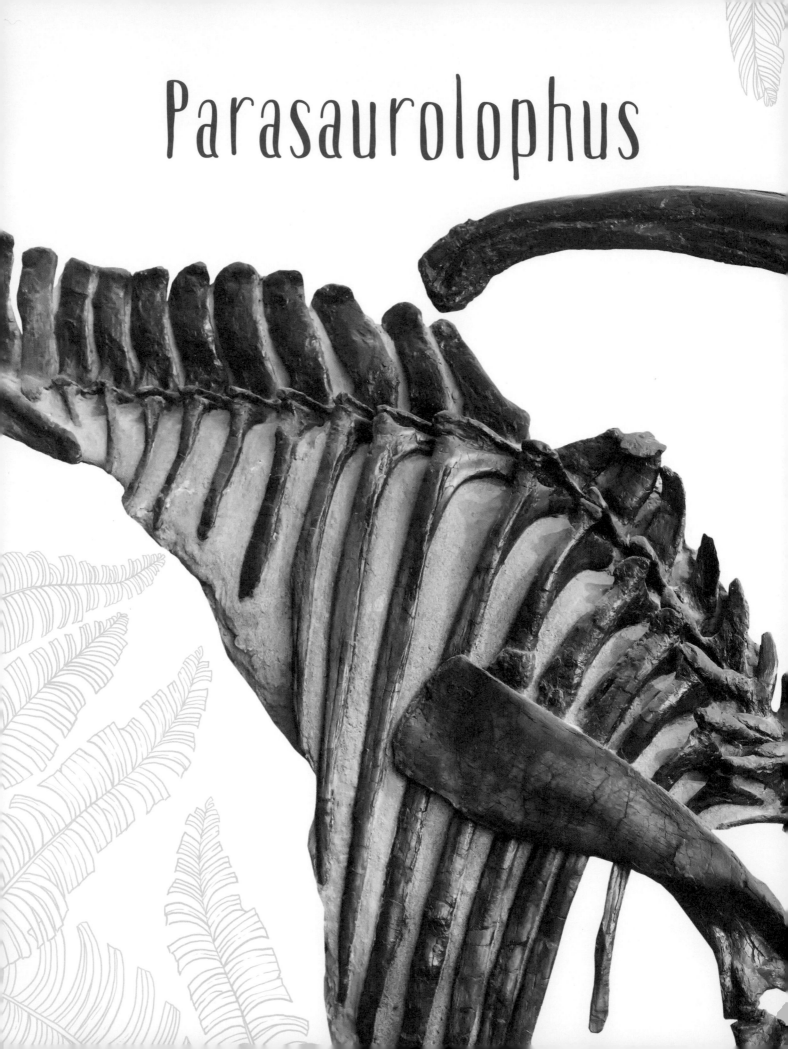

Parasaurolophus

Imagine having a nose as long as three trumpets! Parasaurolophus (PA-ra-SORE-oh-LOAF-us) had just that—a distinctive long crest made from its nose bones that extended backward from its head. We still don't know for sure how the crest was used, but we do have an important clue: it was hollow, like a tube. At first, some paleontologists thought that the crest may have worked like a snorkel to help the dinosaur breathe as it fed on plants underwater 76 million years ago. Now, most agree that Parasaurolophus used it to make sounds to communicate with other members of its herd. This idea is supported by the fact that Parasaurolophus had good hearing.

Including its crest, Parasaurolophus's skull could reach 5 ft (1.6 m) long!

Parasaurolophus. Cretaceous Period, North America.
Fossils of Parasaurolophus show differences in the crest shape and size, possibly between males and females.

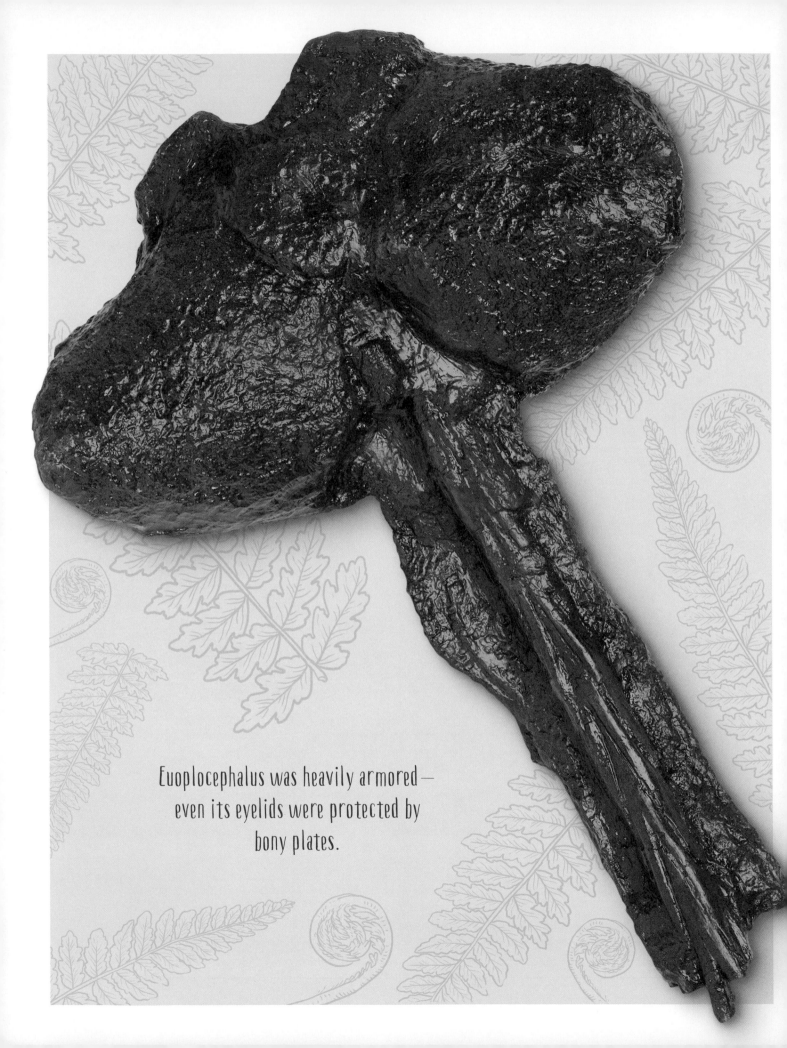

Euoplocephalus was heavily armored—
even its eyelids were protected by
bony plates.

Euoplocephalus

Apart from its legs and belly, every part of tanklike Euoplocephalus (YOU-owe-plo-SEFF-a-lus) was covered with armor. To put off hungry predators, Euoplocephalus had a tough shield of bone covering its back, which was segmented to allow it to move and bend. Rows of spikes made Euoplocephalus look like an even less appetizing meal, and its flexible tail ended in a huge club that it could have slammed into attackers, or possibly rivals for mates.

Euoplocephalus was a plant-eater that lived around 76 million years ago. Recent scans of this dinosaur's skull revealed that it had long, looping passages in its nose, which could have helped it make low sounds. It may have used these noises to communicate.

Euoplocephalus. Cretaceous Period, North America. This bony tail club could have been swung at predators to cause serious injury.

Ornithomimus

Ornithomimus had large eyes, which suggests that it may have been nocturnal (active at night).

Ornithomimus. Cretaceous Period, North America. With its light skeleton and long legs, Ornithomimus was a fast runner.

Does this dinosaur remind you of a large bird like an ostrich or an emu? Othniel Charles Marsh, the American paleontologist who named it, thought so—Ornithomimus (OR-nith-oh-MIME-us) means "bird mimic." At the top of its long neck, Ornithomimus had a small skull with a toothless beak. It was a theropod—a type of dinosaur that usually ate meat—but it is likely that Ornithomimus was an omnivore.

Ornithomimus's thin arms had long feathers on them and its body was covered with more fuzzy feathers. Fossil skin impressions from this 76-million-year-old dinosaur suggest, however, that its legs were bare, making it look even more like an ostrich. Like birds today, its feathers would have kept Ornithomimus snug when the weather was cold.

Velociraptor belonged to a group of dinosaurs called dromaeosaurs, all of which had killer claws.

Velociraptor

About the size of a large dog, Velociraptor (vel-OSS-ee-RAP-tor) may not have been the largest predator, but it was equipped with up to 60 serrated teeth and a razor-sharp "killer claw" on each foot. It prowled the deserts of Asia around 75 million years ago, hunting for smaller reptiles, including other dinosaurs, and mammals to eat.

Although no Velociraptor fossils have been discovered with feathers, bumps called "quill knobs" on its arm bones indicate where feathers were attached. Even though Velociraptor had feathers, it was certainly unable to fly—its arms were far too short! Instead, it may have used its feathers to stay warm, for display, or to keep its eggs cozy.

Velociraptor. Cretaceous Period, Asia. The 3 in (6.5 cm) sickle-shaped killer claw was held off the ground to stop it from becoming blunt.

Archelon was the largest
sea turtle to ever live.

Archelon

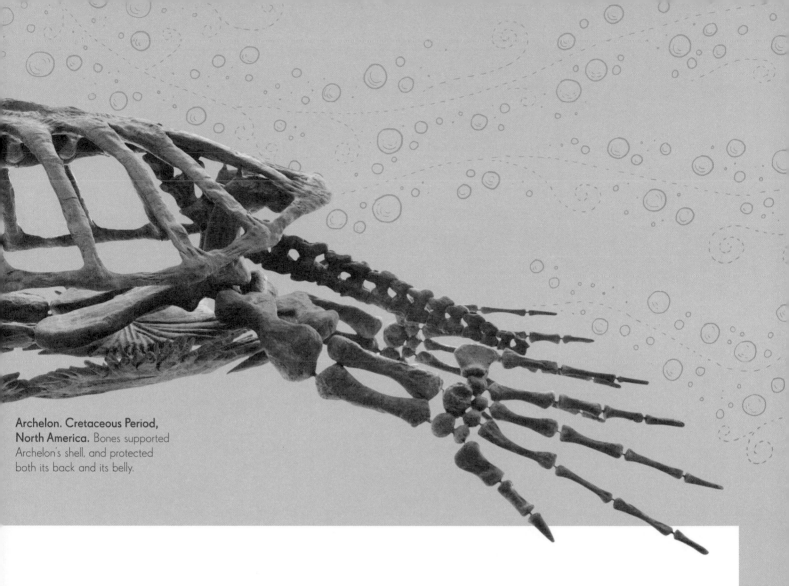

Archelon. Cretaceous Period, North America. Bones supported Archelon's shell, and protected both its back and its belly.

Archelon (ar-kee-LON) was a giant sea turtle the size of a car. Like leatherback sea turtles today, Archelon's outer shell was leathery rather than hard. It couldn't draw its head and legs in like a tortoise can, so its flippers were an easy target for roaming mosasaurs looking for dinner! Archelon lived 75 million years ago and used its huge flippers to paddle through the ocean. It hunted in shallow water, searching for prey on the seafloor. A distinctive hooklike upper beak must have been handy for tearing up soft-bodied prey such as jellyfish, or crunching into shelled invertebrates, such as ammonites. To lay its eggs, Archelon probably had to heave its huge body onto shore, so it could dig a nest in the sand.

Styracosaurus

Styracosaurus (sty-RACK-oh-SORE-us) boasted one of the most elaborate neck frills of any dinosaur. An array of large and small spikes stuck out of the frill, which may have been brightly colored to help Styracosaurus attract a mate. This dinosaur also had sharp horns jutting out of each cheek and an enormous nose horn that could grow to 24 in (60 cm) long. Styracosaurus's collection of horns was probably used as a defense against predators.

Large bone beds—areas filled with fossils—suggest that Styracosaurus lived in large herds around 75 million years ago. It inhabited open plains, and had a strong beak and teeth for cutting and slicing tough vegetation, such as palms and cycads.

Some spikes on Styracosaurus's frill were almost as long as its nose horn!

Styracosaurus. Cretaceous Period, North America. The fan of spikes on Styracosaurus's frill gave it its name, which means "spiked lizard."

Styracosaurus

Some ceratopsians had frills with spikes. Styracosaurus (sty-RACK-oh-SORE-us) had several long spikes that stuck out of its frill, some of which were nearly as long as its nose horn. It lived in North America in the Cretaceous Period.

Thick skull The thick skulls of pachycephalosaurs were often surrounded by smaller spikes.

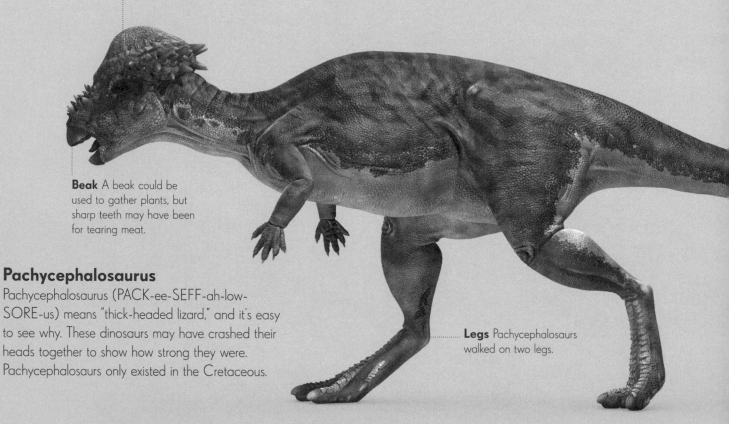

Beak A beak could be used to gather plants, but sharp teeth may have been for tearing meat.

Pachycephalosaurus

Pachycephalosaurus (PACK-ee-SEFF-ah-low-SORE-us) means "thick-headed lizard," and it's easy to see why. These dinosaurs may have crashed their heads together to show how strong they were. Pachycephalosaurs only existed in the Cretaceous.

Legs Pachycephalosaurs walked on two legs.

Psittacosaurus

Psittacosaurus (si-tak-a-SORE-us) was a relatively early ceratopsian that lived in Asia at the beginning of the Cretaceous. It didn't have a frill, but it had a horn on each cheek. The first ceratopsians were small and walked on two legs.

Marginocephalians

Many dinosaurs had unusual characteristics not seen on animals today. The marginocephalians (MAR-jee-no-sa-FAY-lee-ans) had some of the most extravagant features, including spikes, horns, frills, and domed skulls. This large group can be divided into two: the pachycephalosaurs and the ceratopsians. Pachycephalosaurs had thick, bony domes on their heads, which they may have used to ram each other with during fights. The ceratopsians, also known as the "horned dinosaurs," often had large frills on the backs of their heads, as well as long brow and nose horns—this family includes familiar dinosaurs such as Triceratops. Most marginocephalians were herbivores, but some may have eaten small animals.

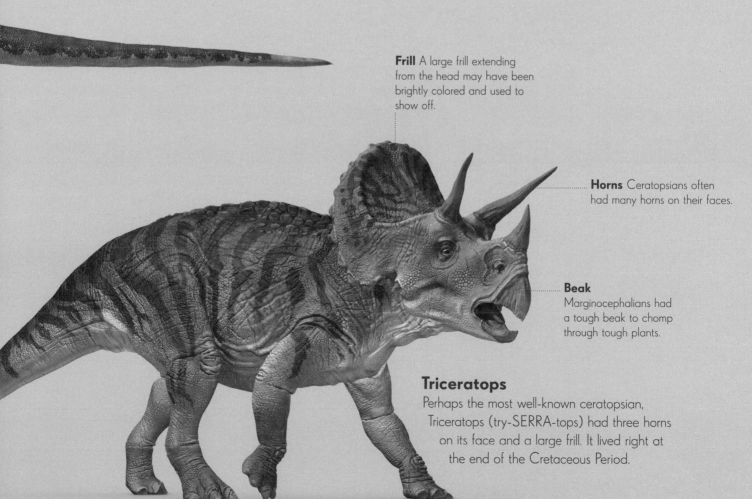

Frill A large frill extending from the head may have been brightly colored and used to show off.

Horns Ceratopsians often had many horns on their faces.

Beak Marginocephalians had a tough beak to chomp through tough plants.

Triceratops
Perhaps the most well-known ceratopsian, Triceratops (try-SERRA-tops) had three horns on its face and a large frill. It lived right at the end of the Cretaceous Period.

Like many birds today, Oviraptor incubated its
eggs and protected them.

Oviraptor

When Oviraptor (OVE-ee-rap-tor) was first discovered, it was found close to a nest of eggs. This inspired its name, which means "egg thief." However, scientists now know that the dinosaur wasn't trying to eat the eggs, but instead to protect them! Oviraptor arranged its eggs in a circle around the nest, with a gap in the middle for it to sit and spread its fluffy feathers over the eggs to keep them warm.

Oviraptor hunted for food in sandy deserts around 75 million years ago. The discovery of a half-digested lizard inside a close relative of Oviraptor suggests that it ate meat, but it may have eaten nuts and seeds as well.

Oviraptor. Cretaceous Period, Asia. Fossils like this show Oviraptor eggs were long and oval-shaped.

Mosasaurs were successful predators that took over the oceans toward the end of the Cretaceous Period.

Plioplatecarpus

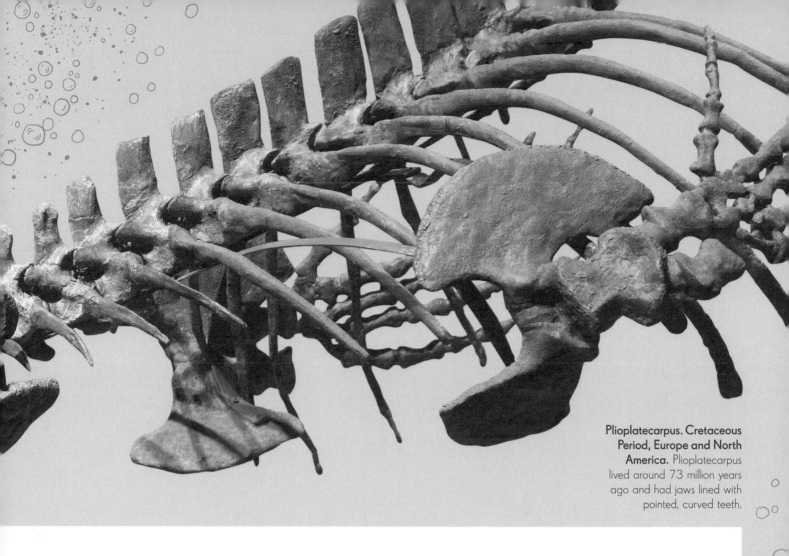

Plioplatecarpus. Cretaceous Period, Europe and North America. Plioplatecarpus lived around 73 million years ago and had jaws lined with pointed, curved teeth.

Plioplatecarpus (PLY-oh-PLAT-ee-CAR-pus) was a ferocious mosasaur. This group of marine reptiles looked very similar to pliosaurs, with long skulls filled with sharp teeth, and short limbs that had webs of skin between their fingers and toes to form paddles. Plioplatecarpus had a long tail and it used it to propel itself through the water to chase after prey. Like a snake, its jaws had a double hinge, enabling it to open its mouth sideways as well as up and down, which meant it could swallow most prey whole! If you look carefully at some ammonites, you'll see circular puncture marks in their shells that match the teeth of mosasaurs—proof that they were a favorite crunchy snack.

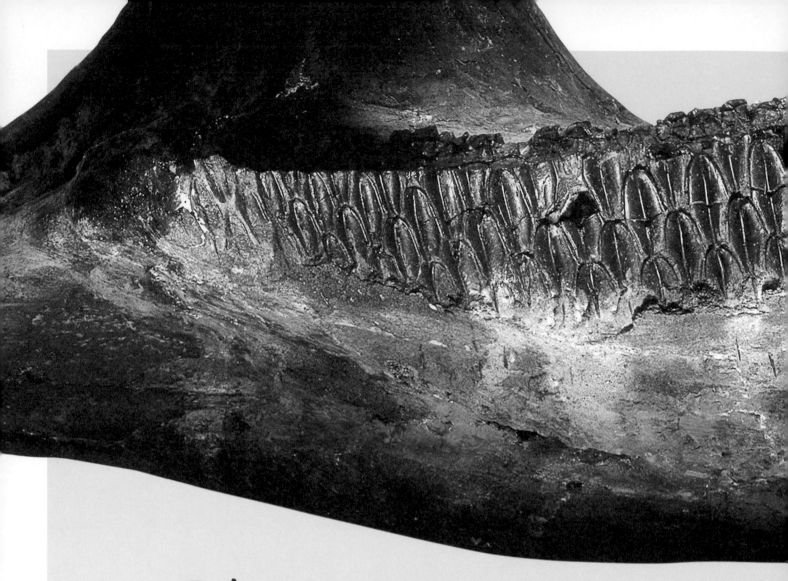

Edmontosaurus

Many Edmontosaurus bones show bite marks,
probably made by Tyrannosaurus.

Known from several sites and thousands of fossilized bones,
Edmontosaurus (ed-MONT-oh-SORE-us) is one of the most
well-studied dinosaurs. Even mummified remains and impressions of
its skin have been discovered. Edmontosaurus was a duck-billed
dinosaur that plodded around the warm forests of North America
from around 73 million years ago. It had a broad beak at the front
of its snout to snip off conifer needles, twigs, and bark, which was
chewed up with the many teeth that lined its jaws.

Studies of Edmontosaurus fossils collected from within the Arctic
Circle show that, surprisingly, instead of migrating, these dinosaurs
stayed put all year round. How did they survive the long, dark,
cooler winter? Scientists aren't yet sure.

Long fingers and claws gave Deinocheirus its name,
which means "terrible hand" in ancient Greek.

Deinocheirus

For more than 50 years, all that was known of Deinocheirus (DINO-ky-russ) was a pair of gigantic arms ending in huge claws, each of which was longer than a banana! In 2013, fossils of the rest of Deinocheirus's skeleton were discovered—and they revealed a truly bizarre animal. This dinosaur was 36 ft (11 m) long, and in addition to its fearsome claws, it had a humped back, feathers, and a toothless beak. The beak suggests that Deinocheirus ate plants, and many small stones, called gastroliths, were found in its stomach; these would have helped it to grind up tough vegetation. Its belly, however, also contained the remains of fish, suggesting it was an omnivore. Deinocheirus lived around 70 million years ago.

Deinocheirus. Cretaceous Period, Asia. These Deinocheirus arms were found in Mongolia and are 8 ft (2.5 m) long. It used them to gather plants and catch fish, and to defend itself from predators.

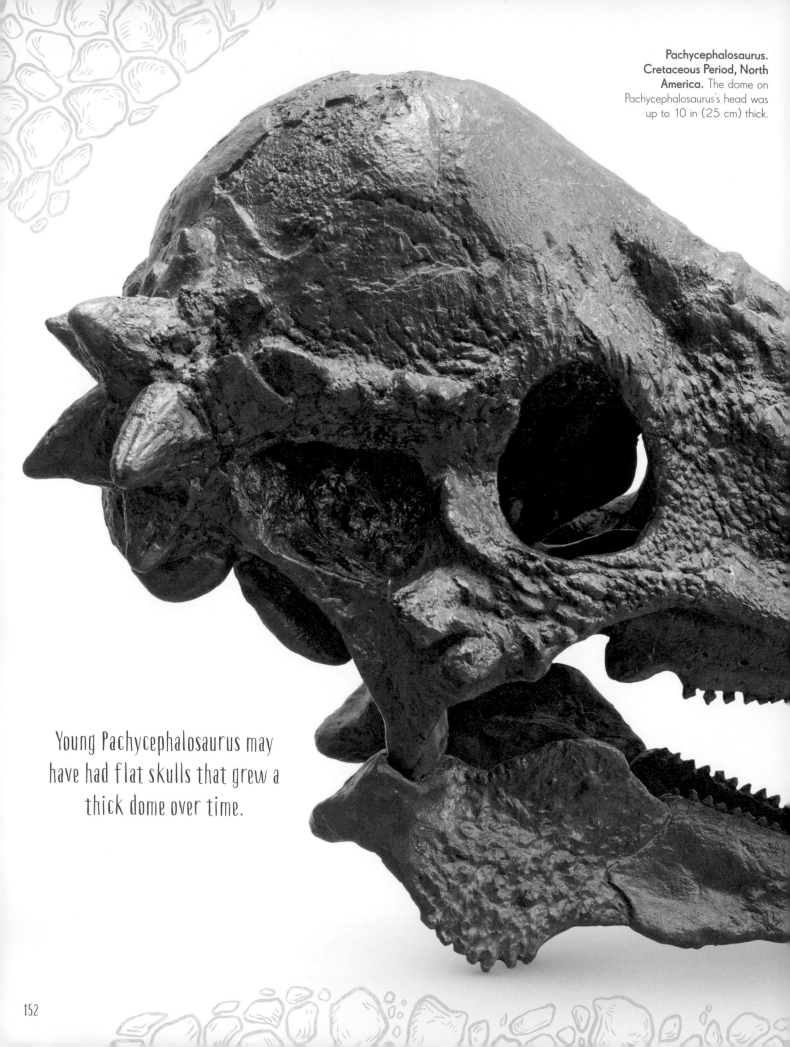

Pachycephalosaurus. Cretaceous Period, North America. The dome on Pachycephalosaurus's head was up to 10 in (25 cm) thick.

Young Pachycephalosaurus may have had flat skulls that grew a thick dome over time.

Pachycephalosaurus

rash! You wouldn't want to get in the way of a fighting Pachycephalosaurus (PACK-ee-SEFF-ah-low-SORE-us) and its rival. This dinosaur was closely related to the ceratopsians, such as Triceratops, but instead of a frill that extended from its head, it had a distinctive thick, bony skull. These dome-headed dinosaurs are thought to have rammed into one another with their heads—like head-butting bighorn sheep do today—to impress mates. Many Pachycephalosaurus skulls show damage that may have been caused by clashing together.

Pachycephalosaurus existed about 70 million years ago. It walked on two legs and had large eyes, which helped it to see well. This dinosaur probably ate plants, but its sharp teeth suggest it might also have eaten some unlucky small animals, too.

Fossils of young and old Triceratops show that as they grew, their frill and horns grew much longer.

Triceratops. Cretaceous Period, North America. From the tip of its beak to the back of its frill, a Triceratops' skull could measure a whopping 8 ft (2.5 m).

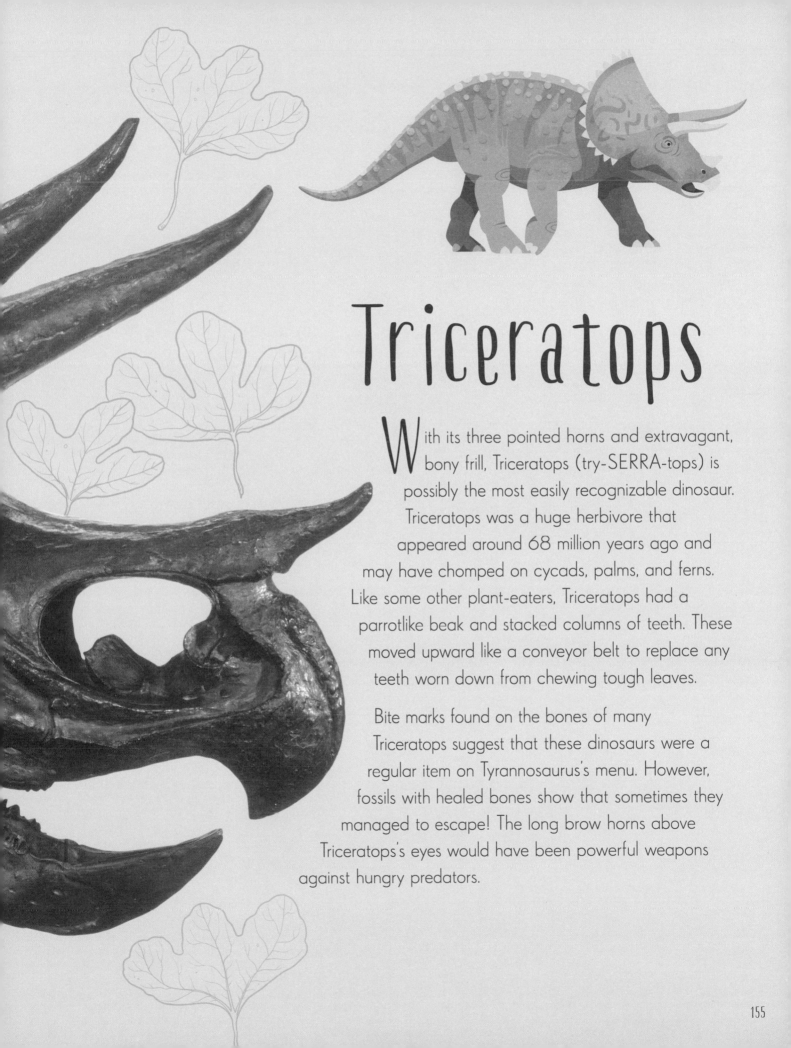

Triceratops

With its three pointed horns and extravagant, bony frill, Triceratops (try-SERRA-tops) is possibly the most easily recognizable dinosaur. Triceratops was a huge herbivore that appeared around 68 million years ago and may have chomped on cycads, palms, and ferns. Like some other plant-eaters, Triceratops had a parrotlike beak and stacked columns of teeth. These moved upward like a conveyor belt to replace any teeth worn down from chewing tough leaves.

Bite marks found on the bones of many Triceratops suggest that these dinosaurs were a regular item on Tyrannosaurus's menu. However, fossils with healed bones show that sometimes they managed to escape! The long brow horns above Triceratops's eyes would have been powerful weapons against hungry predators.

Tyrannosaurus

Instantly recognizable from its gigantic body and tiny arms, Tyrannosaurus (TIE-ran-oh-SORE-us) is probably the most famous dinosaur. Reaching up to 43 ft (13 m) long, it was among the biggest predators to ever live. Tyrannosaurus stomped around the forests of Cretaceous North America, around 68 million years ago, looking for food. This dinosaur's fearsome teeth were capable of chomping huge mouthfuls of meat—the equivalent of 4,000 sausages in one bite—and even splitting apart bones. Many herbivorous dinosaur fossils show Tyrannosaurus bite marks, but broken and healed Tyrannosaurus bones show that sometimes its prey fought back! An easier meal for hungry Tyrannosaurus was to scavenge food left behind by other predators.

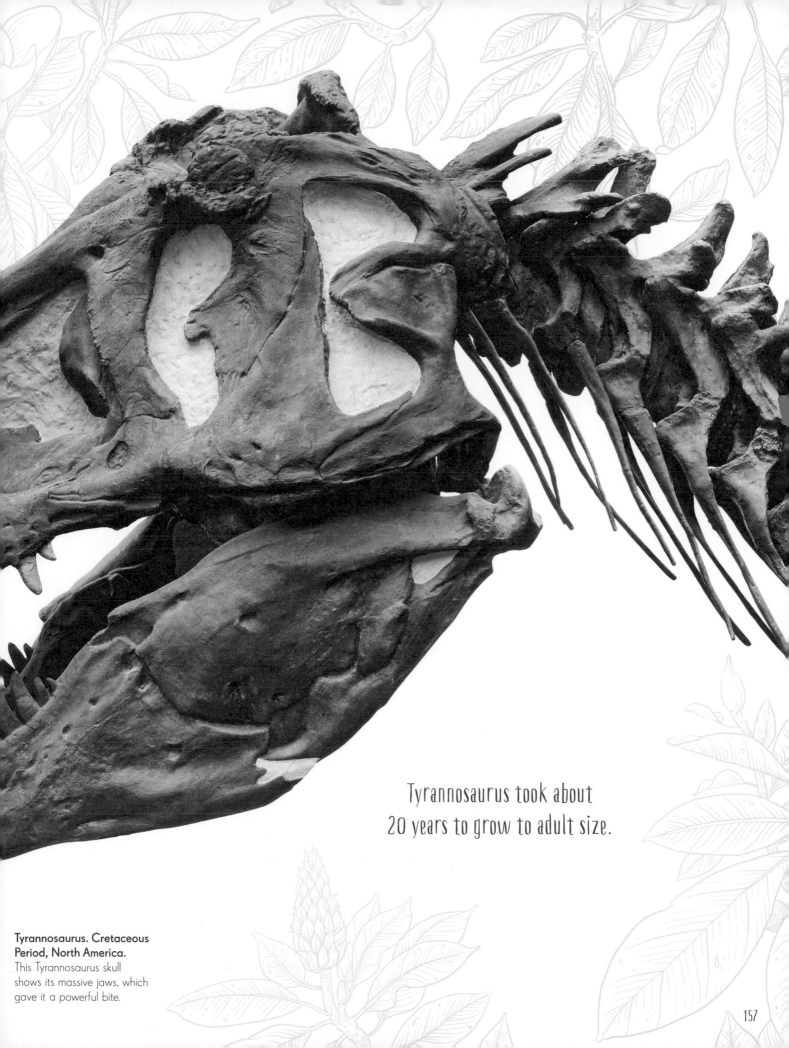

Tyrannosaurus took about
20 years to grow to adult size.

**Tyrannosaurus. Cretaceous
Period, North America.**
This Tyrannosaurus skull
shows its massive jaws, which
gave it a powerful bite.

Paleogene Period (66–23 MYA)

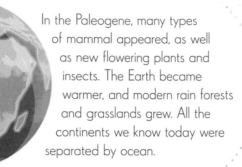

In the Paleogene, many types of mammal appeared, as well as new flowering plants and insects. The Earth became warmer, and modern rain forests and grasslands grew. All the continents we know today were separated by ocean.

Quaternary Period (2 MYA–present)

Earth's climate cooled in the Quaternary, which led to an ice age. The changing climate as well as human hunting meant many larger animals became extinct. The continents moved to where they are today.

Neogene Period (23–2 MYA)

Grasslands flourished in the Neogene, and seaweed forests thrived in the ocean. Some of the continents, including North and South America, joined together, which allowed organisms to move between them. In Africa, early humans appeared.

Cenozoic Era

66 Million Years Ago (MYA)—present

After the extinction of the non-bird dinosaurs, at the end of the Mesozoic Era, mammals had new opportunites to spread. They soon dominated the land, and the Cenozoic Era is also known as the "Age of Mammals." During this time, the continents moved to their current locations and, although temperatures rose at the beginning of the Cenozoic, dramatic cooling then resulted in a series of ice ages. This era saw the appearance of many mammals that still exist today, including humans, but also the extinction of larger prehistoric beasts. The Cenozoic is divided into three periods: the Paleogene, Neogene, and Quaternary.

Nummulite

This small, disk-shaped organism is called a nummulite (NUM-you-light), which means "little coin." It is a type of foraminiferan, which are single-celled organisms with hard outer shells usually found in the mud and sand of the seafloor. Around 56 million years ago, nummulites thrived in what was a huge shallow sea called the Tethys Ocean. In its warm waters, the biggest nummulites may have lived for up to 100 years and reached 6 in (16 cm) across—for a life-form made of just one cell, that's gigantic!

Nummulite shells are often found in rocks where the Tethys Ocean used to be. Their fossils can be seen in the limestone blocks used by the ancient Egyptians to build the pyramids.

Nummulites still live on the seafloor today, but they only grow to about the length of a small ant.

Nummulite. Paleogene Period to present, Worldwide. This circular nummulite shell has slightly worn away to reveal the tiny, spirally arranged chambers within it.

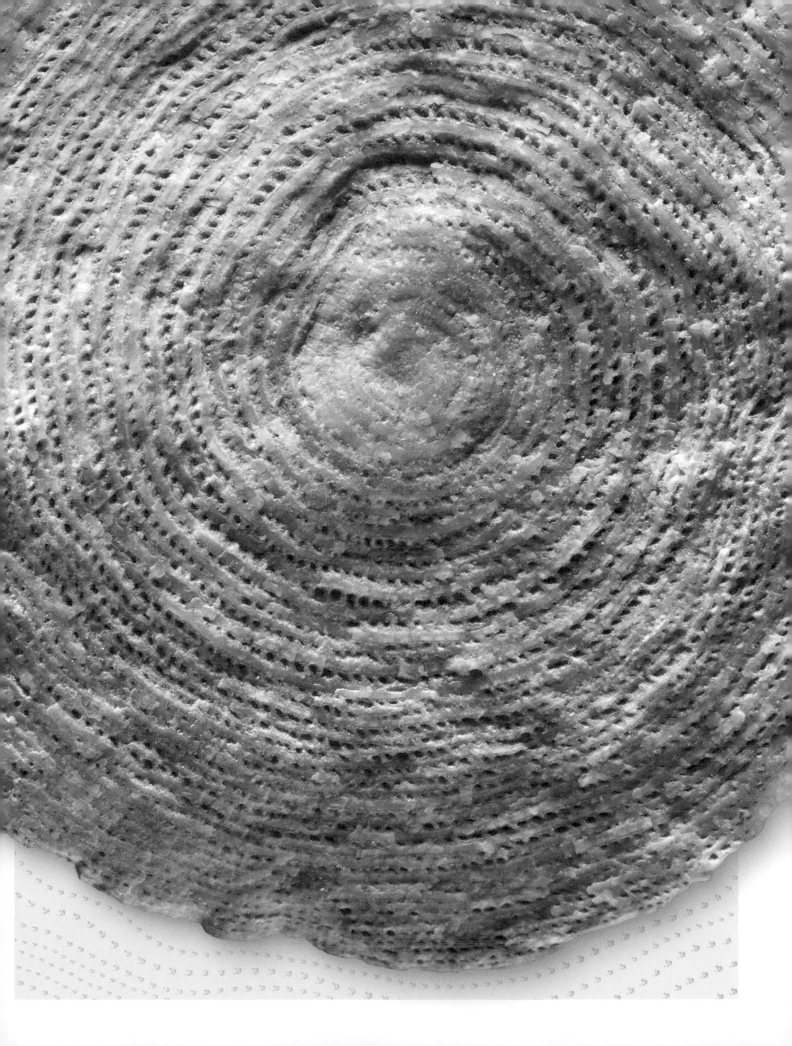

Titanoboa. Paleogene Period, South America.
A single vertebra (part of the backbone) of Titanoboa like this is more than three times the size of that of a modern boa constrictor.

Titanoboa was the largest snake that has ever lived.

Titanoboa

As long as a school bus and so wide it couldn't fit through a door, this terrifying snake ruled the swamps of South America about 7 million years after the extinction event that wiped out non-bird dinosaurs. It was not poisonous, but that would have been no comfort to its prey, since Titanoboa (tie-TAN-oh-BO-ah) was a constrictor that crushed its victims in the coils of its powerful body. Titanoboa lived alongside giant turtles and crocodiles, which it may have eaten, along with large fish. Like modern anacondas, this snake probably swam through rivers to hunt. The warm tropical climate when Titanoboa lived likely made it possible for the reptiles to grow to giant sizes, as these cold-blooded animals found it easier to stay warm.

Heliobatis

Heliobatis means "sun ray" — it is named after its fossilized fins, which fan out like sunbeams.

Gliding along underwater, Heliobatis (he-lee-oh-BAT-iss) looked very similar to a modern ray. However, unlike most rays today, it preferred freshwater lakes and rivers to the saltwater sea. By rippling the edges of its circular body, Heliobatis could swim smoothly above the muddy floor, hunting for food. Smaller fish and crayfish were its target. It crunched them up with the sharp teeth in its mouth, which was hidden on its underside.

Rays are related to sharks, and both have a covering of tough scales, as well as flexible skeletons made of cartilage—the bendy material found in your nose and ears. Heliobatis also had up to three menacing spines on its long tail—it may even have been able to inject venom with them.

Heliobatis. Paleogene Period, North America. This Heliobatis from Wyoming was fossilized alongside some Knightia (NITE-ee-ah) fish.

Mene

Mene (MEE-nee) fish first appeared in the Paleogene Period, around 55 million years ago, but they can still be found in the sea! One species—also known as a moonfish because of its round, shiny body—lives in the Indian and Pacific oceans today. Prehistoric Mene could grow to about 12 in (30 cm) long and had a very similar body shape to modern Mene. These unusual fish have a very large stomach and two long, thin fins on their tummies. Without large fins at its sides, Mene has to drive itself through the water using its tailfin, but its flat body helps it cut through the water. In modern Mene, the tail is forked, but fossil Mene had a triangular tail.

A fossil site in Italy is known as "the fishbowl" because so many fossil fish are found there, including many Mene.

Mene. Paleogene Period to present, Worldwide. This amazingly well-preserved Mene fossil even shows the thin fins on its stomach.

Florissantia is a type of mallow plant,
which means it is related to the plant
from which we make chocolate.

Florissantia

Florissantia (FLOOR-i-SAN-tee-a) was an extinct plant that lived during much of the Paleogene Period, and it is known from many fossils of parts of flowers, fruit, and even grains of pollen. This fossil may look like a delicate flower, but it's not quite as it seems. It actually shows the petal-like shapes of the sepals—a special type of leaf—that usually protect the flower at their center. Only one species of Florissantia had petals, which are rarely preserved. Florissantia's flowers grew on long stalks, and the various parts of the flower were present in fives—with five petals, five sepals, and five stamens that produced pollen. No fossils of the leaves have been found, so no one knows what the whole plant looked like.

Florissantia. Paleogene Period, North America. This fossil shows the five sepals, and the veins within them that food and water would have flowed through.

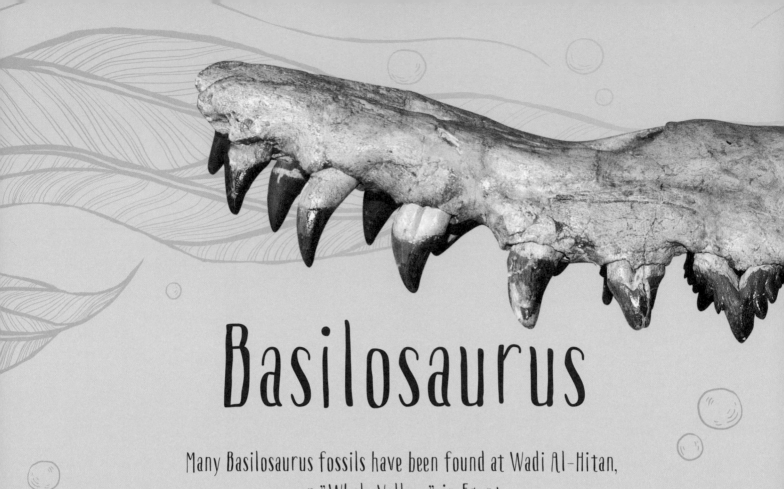

Basilosaurus

Many Basilosaurus fossils have been found at Wadi Al-Hitan, or "Whale Valley," in Egypt.

Basilosaurus. Paleogene Period, Africa and North America.
Basilosaurus had pointed teeth at the front of its jaws and serrated teeth at the back.

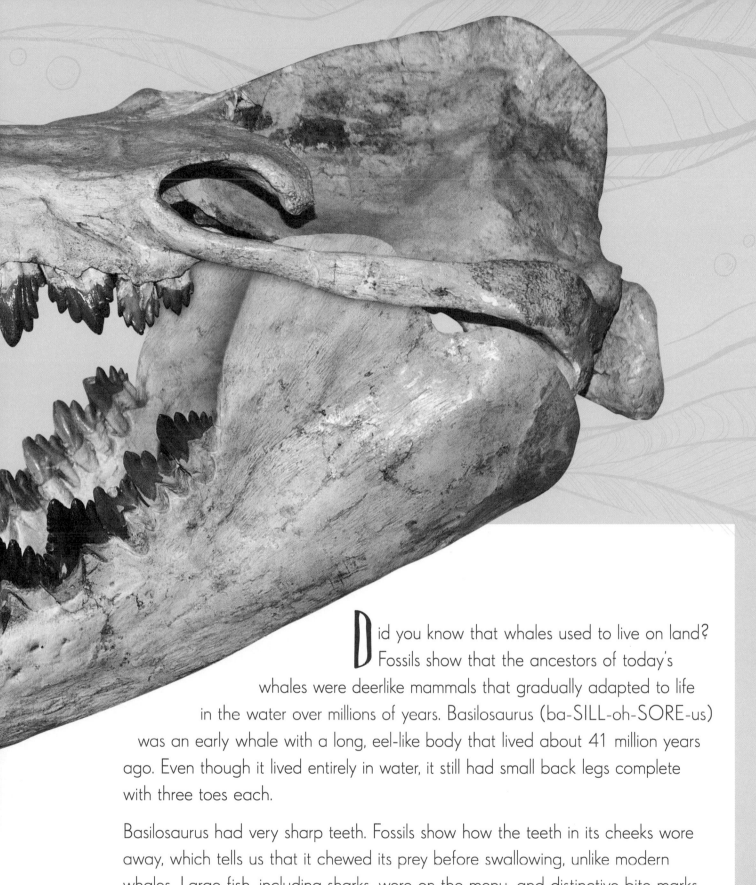

Did you know that whales used to live on land? Fossils show that the ancestors of today's whales were deerlike mammals that gradually adapted to life in the water over millions of years. Basilosaurus (ba-SILL-oh-SORE-us) was an early whale with a long, eel-like body that lived about 41 million years ago. Even though it lived entirely in water, it still had small back legs complete with three toes each.

Basilosaurus had very sharp teeth. Fossils show how the teeth in its cheeks wore away, which tells us that it chewed its prey before swallowing, unlike modern whales. Large fish, including sharks, were on the menu, and distinctive bite marks on young Dorudon—a close relative of Basilosaurus—suggest that it even ate other whales.

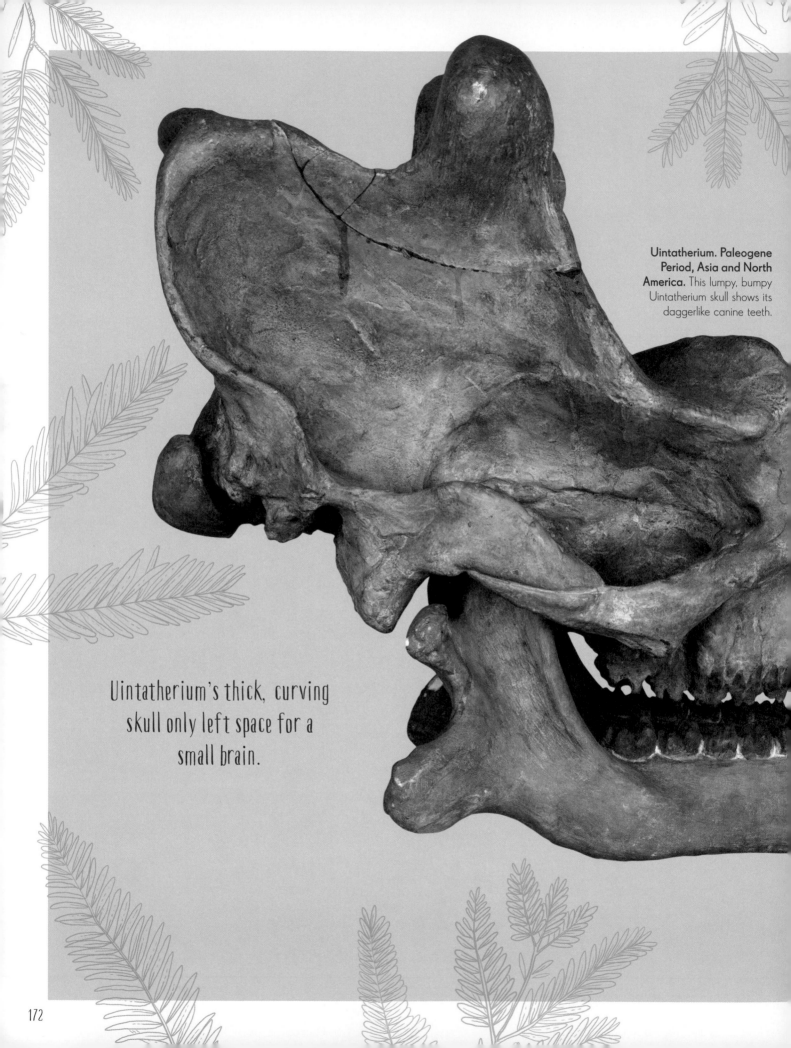

Uintatherium. Paleogene Period, Asia and North America. This lumpy, bumpy Uintatherium skull shows its daggerlike canine teeth.

Uintatherium's thick, curving skull only left space for a small brain.

Uintatherium

Although unrelated to rhinos, Uintatherium (win-tah-THEE-ree-um) was similar in size and shape. However, it had a very unusually shaped head. Male Uintatherium had three pairs of horns and two giant, bladelike canine teeth, which are thought to have been used to attract mates. This large mammal lived 40 million years ago and, despite its fearsome teeth, it chomped only on plants.

In the US in the late 1800s, Uintatherium's bizarre-looking fossils were caught up in the "Bone Wars." At this time, there was a rush to name new prehistoric animals and two paleontologists in particular, Othniel Charles Marsh and Edward Drinker Cope, kept naming new species from fossils that all turned out to belong to Uintatherium!

Archaeotherium. Paleogene Period, North America.
Archaeotherium's skull measured up to 3 ft (1m) long and contained many sharp, interlocking teeth.

Fossil evidence suggests Archaeotherium preyed on early camels and piled up their carcasses to eat later!

Archaeotherium

Shady forests were home to Archaeotherium (ar-kee-oh-THEER-ee-um) when it lived about 30 million years ago. It looked like a colossal pig, but it was more closely related to whales and hippos. Its large head was held up by strong neck muscles that attached to long bones above its shoulders—and a big head meant it could have a big mouth! Archaeotherium's huge pointed canines and wide molar teeth could crush and tear almost any food, and this mammal was most likely an unfussy omnivore. It had a good sense of smell, and its forward-pointing eyes were able to accurately pinpoint how far away its prey was. The bony lumps on its head may have been for showing off to other Archaeotherium.

Amber

The oldest pieces of amber with animals preserved inside are 230 million years old.

Amber is the fossilized remains of sticky resin that oozes out of pine trees. The trees make the resin to seal up wounds when they are damaged. It's not surprising that insects and other small creatures occasionally get stuck in the gummy liquid, which drips down the tree bark. These events are unlucky for the animals, but lucky for scientists, because the resin then hardens and perfectly preserves anything inside. Each piece of amber is like a little time capsule—the wings of baby Mesozoic birds, dinosaur feathers, and even a whole lizard have been frozen in time for us to see. This blob of amber captured a tiny gnat 30 million years ago, and it still looks as if the winged creepy-crawly could fly away at any moment.

Phorusrhacos and its relatives are commonly known as "terror birds"!

Phorusrhacos

Like a supersized eagle, Phorusrhacos (FOR-us-RAH-koss) had a large, sharply curved beak that could tear into meat easily. Luckily for its prey, this huge bird couldn't fly, but it was still a terrifying predator that stood as tall as an ostrich and could run quicker than the fastest human sprinter. Its long, powerful legs could also give a hefty, defensive kick, but there weren't many animals that would try to attack a Phorusrhacos—it was one of the top carnivores in South America, where it lived 20 million years ago. In addition to its vicious beak, Phorusrhacos's toes each had a sharp claw, and it used its fearsome weaponry to bring down mammals as big as deer.

Phorusrhacos. Neogene Period, South America.
Phorusrhacos's upper beak was armed with a sharp, curved point.

Megalodons and great white sharks
lived side by side for several million years, but
megalodons were about three times bigger.

Megalodon

Megalodons (MEG-a-LO-dons) ruled the warm seas in the Neogene Period. At up to 60 ft (18 m) long, they were the largest sharks that have ever lived and were the top ocean predators until their extinction around 4 million years ago. With massive jaws lined with 276 huge teeth, and a serious appetite, this ferocious fish probably ate any unlucky animal it came across, including whales and other sharks. Some fossilized whale bones have megalodon bite marks in them.

The scientific name for megalodons is Otodus (oh-TOE-dus), which means "ear-shaped tooth." Since a megalodon's skeleton was mainly made of soft cartilage, like our noses, only its teeth and sometimes parts of its dinner-plate-size backbones have been preserved as fossils.

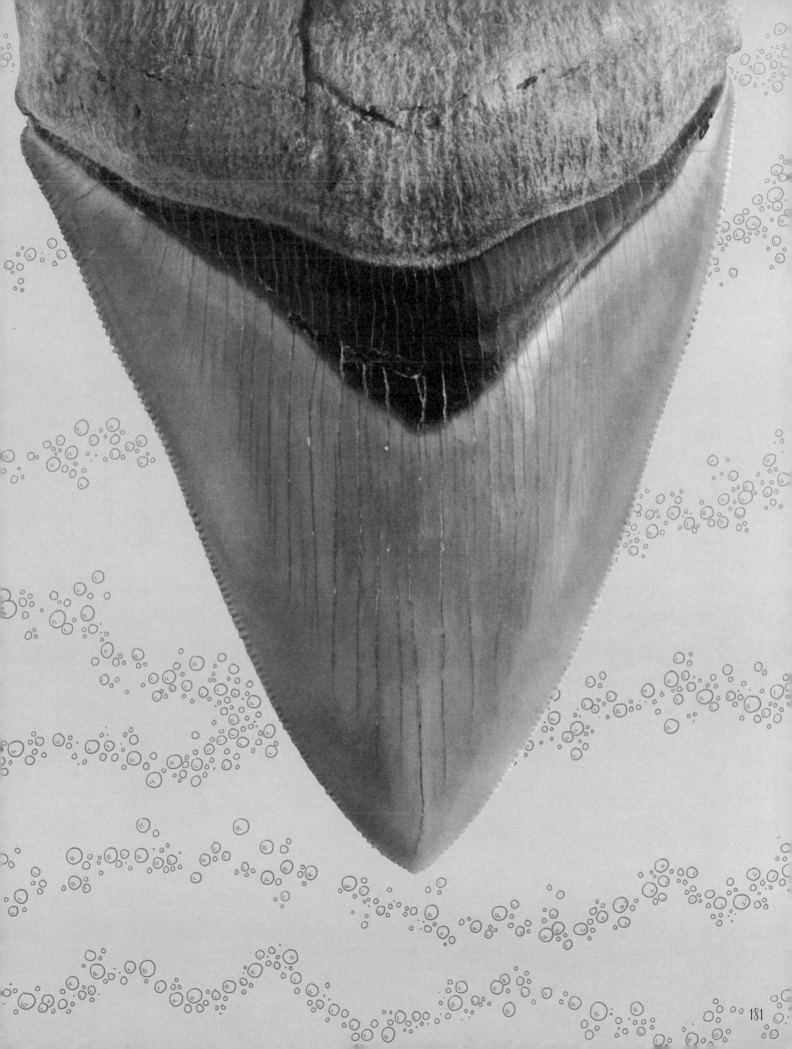

The upper tusks of Gomphotherium could be 6½ ft (2 m) long!

Gomphotherium

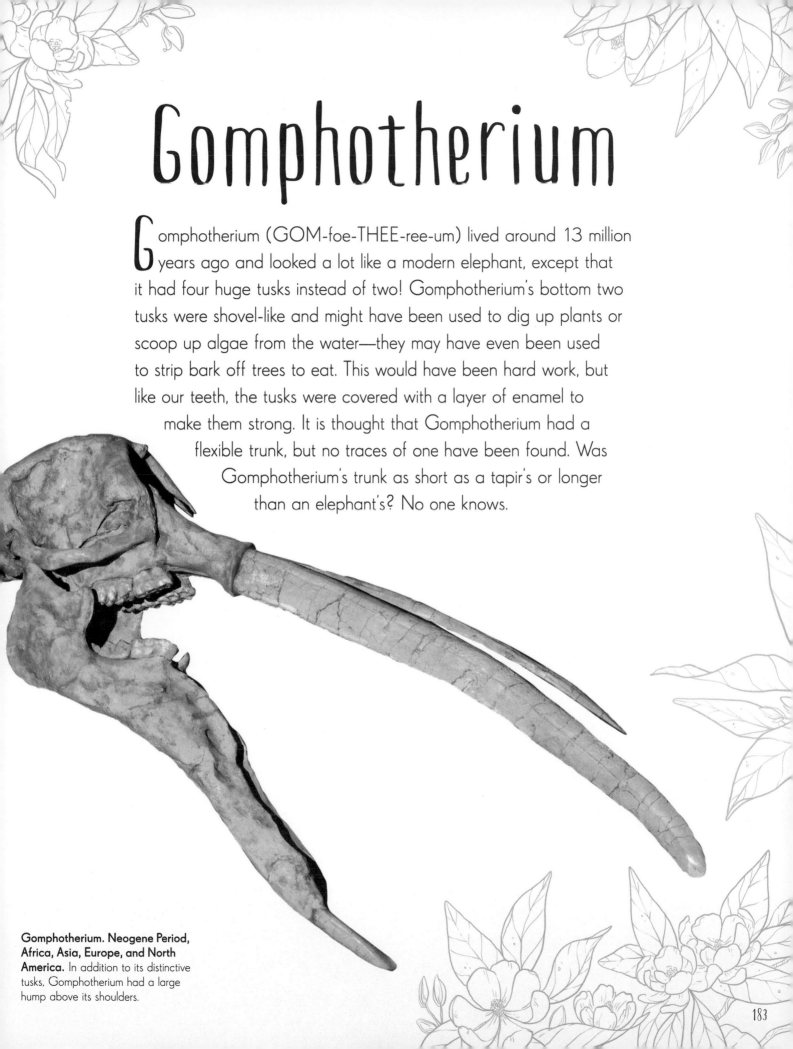

Gomphotherium (GOM-foe-THEE-ree-um) lived around 13 million years ago and looked a lot like a modern elephant, except that it had four huge tusks instead of two! Gomphotherium's bottom two tusks were shovel-like and might have been used to dig up plants or scoop up algae from the water—they may have even been used to strip bark off trees to eat. This would have been hard work, but like our teeth, the tusks were covered with a layer of enamel to make them strong. It is thought that Gomphotherium had a flexible trunk, but no traces of one have been found. Was Gomphotherium's trunk as short as a tapir's or longer than an elephant's? No one knows.

Gomphotherium. Neogene Period, Africa, Asia, Europe, and North America. In addition to its distinctive tusks, Gomphotherium had a large hump above its shoulders.

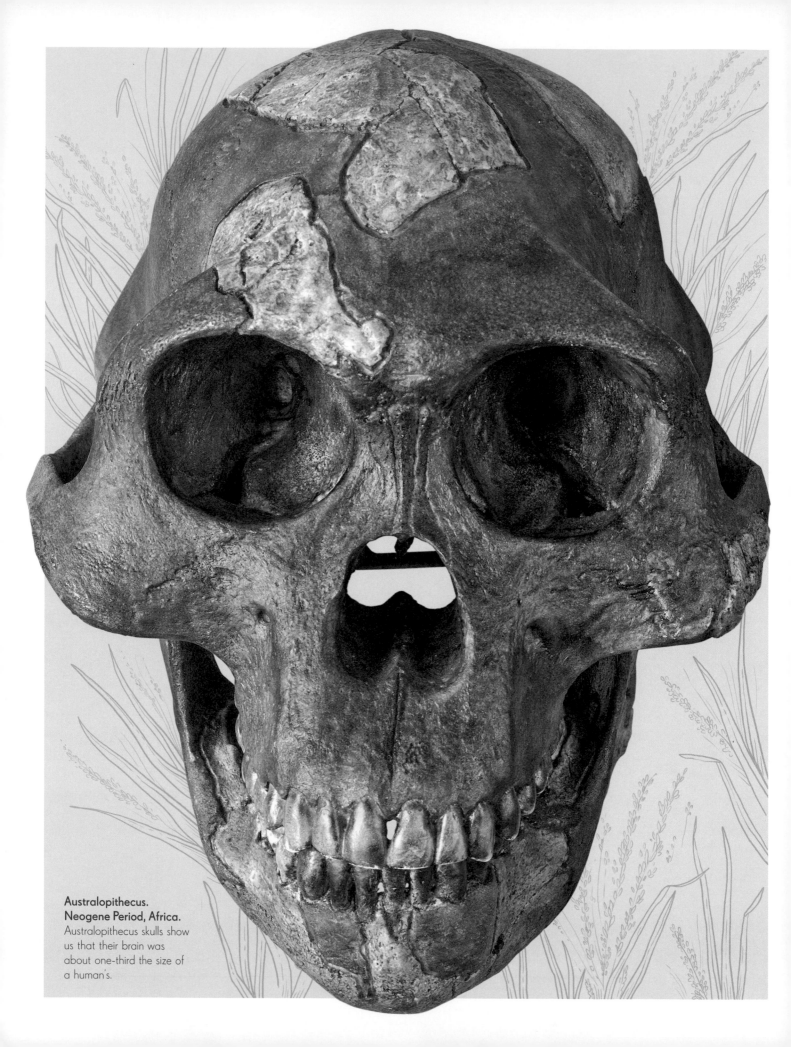

**Australopithecus.
Neogene Period, Africa.**
Australopithecus skulls show
us that their brain was
about one-third the size of
a human's.

Australopithecus

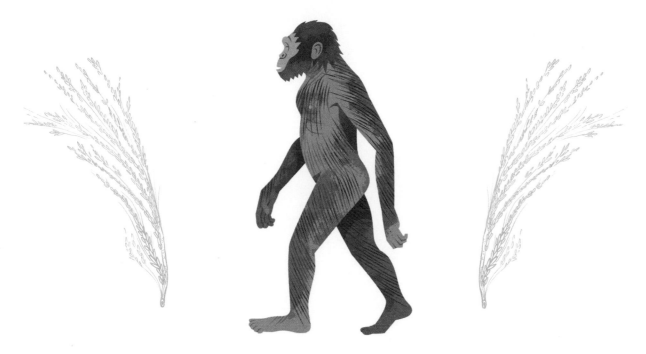

Australopithecus fossils have been found in eastern and southern Africa.

We can learn a lot about human evolution from fossils. Australopithecus (OSS-tra-low-PITH-ee-cuss) was not a human, but it was an early ancestor of humans that appeared around 4 million years ago. Its fossils show a mix of apelike and humanlike features. For example, it had a small brain like an ape, but it walked on two legs, like humans do. Australopithecus probably ate a wide range of foods, from fruits to animals, and it may even have used stone tools to cut them up.

In 1976, scientist Mary Leakey discovered a trail of fossilized Australopithecus footprints in Tanzania, and in 2015 more were uncovered. The tracks suggest that Australopithecus lived in groups.

Coelodonta

Frozen remains and cave paintings by early humans give us a good idea of how Coelodonta (SEE-low-DON-tah), also known as the woolly rhinoceros, looked. Like the mammoths they lived with, woolly rhinoceroses were covered in thick, long hair to keep them warm in the freezing temperatures of the Ice Age. They also had small ears to reduce heat loss and a large hump on their shoulders to store fat, which was used as an energy reserve when there was no food available.

The woolly rhinoceros may have used its long nose horn to defend itself or to fight rivals for mates. When its horns were first discovered, some people believed they were claws belonging to a giant bird.

In 2020, a frozen woolly rhinoceros that had some of its internal organs preserved was discovered in Russia in melting ice!

Coelodonta. Neogene to Quaternary periods, Asia and Europe. Woolly rhinoceroses had two horns. The larger one on their nose could reach 5 ft (1.4 m) long.

Ice ages

Over its immense history, the Earth's climate has changed—from the tropical temperatures of the Triassic Period to the Ice Age of the Quaternary. What caused these changes in climate? The moving continents, volcanic eruptions, and the growth of plants may all have contributed. Ice ages are periods when the Earth is cooler and sheets of ice permanently cover parts of the globe. During the most recent ice age, also known as the "Ice Age," animals had to adapt to life in the cold. However, rising temperatures and other factors such as hunting meant many of these animals became extinct.

Snowball Earth
About 700 million years ago, the Earth twice became so cold that it was completely covered in snow and ice. This is known as a "snowball Earth"! Only single-celled organisms could survive in this harsh climate.

The Ice Age
The Ice Age is still going on today! At its coldest, about 21,000 years ago, much of the northern hemisphere was covered in snow, but now only the Arctic and Antarctic are always icy.

Ancient bison

This big herbivore was an ancestor of the American bison. The ancient bison, Bison antiquus (BYE-son an-TICK-yoo-uss) lived in North America and became extinct 10,000 years ago.

Cave lion

Until it became extinct around 13,000 years ago, the cave lion, Panthera spelaea (PAN-theer-RA spe-LEE-a), was a top Ice Age predator. It was closely related to modern lions, although it had no mane.

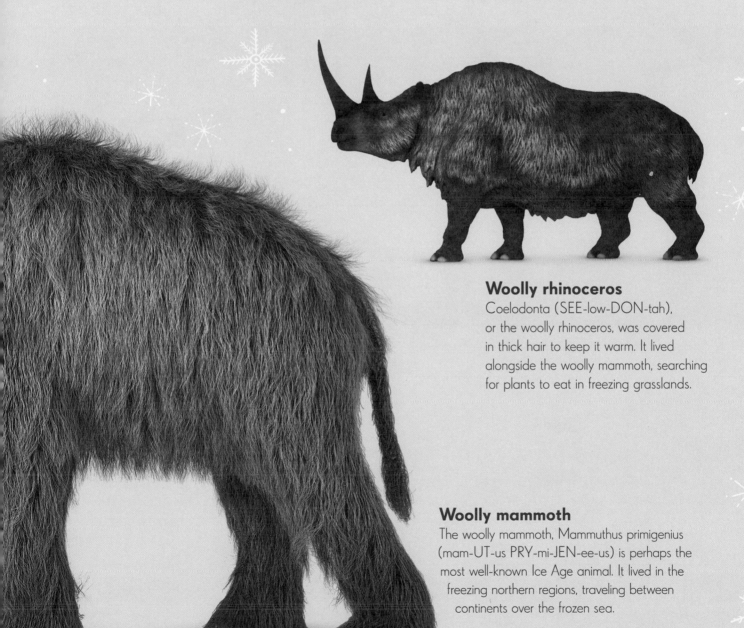

Woolly rhinoceros

Coelodonta (SEE-low-DON-tah), or the woolly rhinoceros, was covered in thick hair to keep it warm. It lived alongside the woolly mammoth, searching for plants to eat in freezing grasslands.

Woolly mammoth

The woolly mammoth, Mammuthus primigenius (mam-UT-us PRY-mi-JEN-ee-us) is perhaps the most well-known Ice Age animal. It lived in the freezing northern regions, traveling between continents over the frozen sea.

Glyptodon

Early humans may have used empty Glyptodon shells to shelter inside.

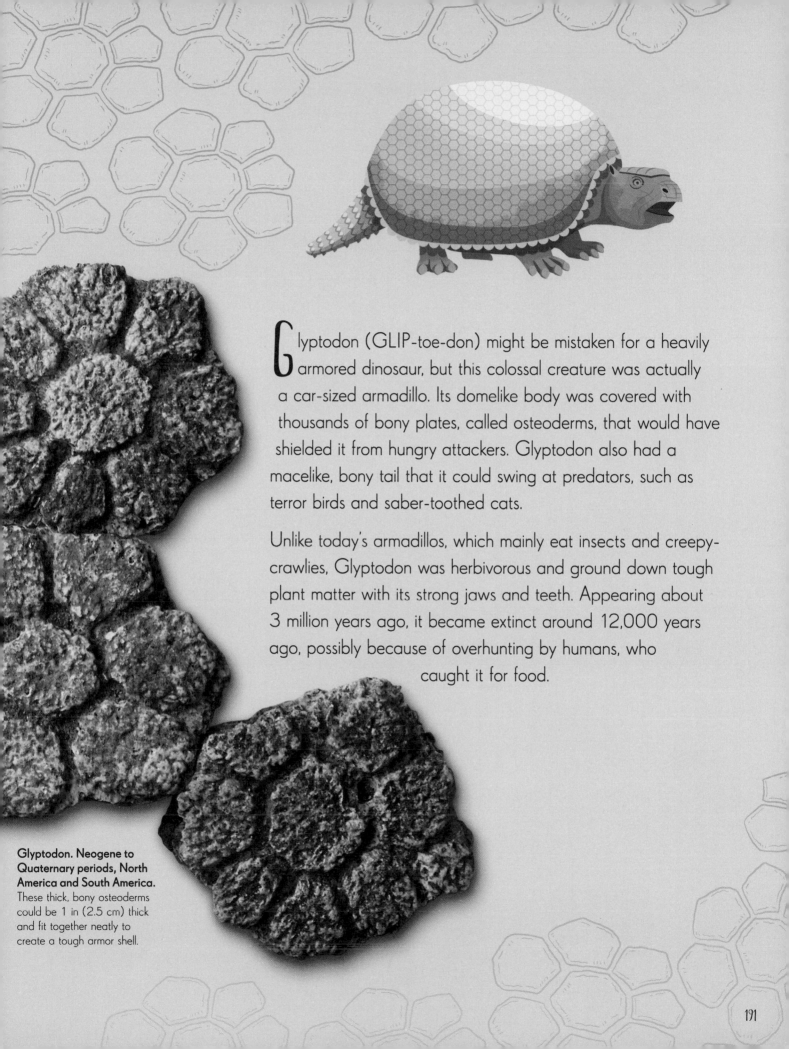

Glyptodon (GLIP-toe-don) might be mistaken for a heavily armored dinosaur, but this colossal creature was actually a car-sized armadillo. Its domelike body was covered with thousands of bony plates, called osteoderms, that would have shielded it from hungry attackers. Glyptodon also had a macelike, bony tail that it could swing at predators, such as terror birds and saber-toothed cats.

Unlike today's armadillos, which mainly eat insects and creepy-crawlies, Glyptodon was herbivorous and ground down tough plant matter with its strong jaws and teeth. Appearing about 3 million years ago, it became extinct around 12,000 years ago, possibly because of overhunting by humans, who caught it for food.

Glyptodon. Neogene to Quaternary periods, North America and South America. These thick, bony osteoderms could be 1 in (2.5 cm) thick and fit together neatly to create a tough armor shell.

Smilodon

It's a good thing that Smilodon (SMILE-oh-don) didn't have to brush its teeth—with canines up to 10 in (25 cm) long, it would have taken a while! Smilodon, also known as a saber-toothed cat because of its swordlike teeth, was a formidable prehistoric predator. It lived between 2.5 million to 10,000 years ago in forests, quietly stalking its prey—most likely deer, bison, and even ground sloths. Slinking through the undergrowth, it waited for the perfect moment to pounce on its unsuspecting prey. Smilodon's jaws could open twice as wide as that of a modern lion to deliver a deadly bite. However, Smilodon wasn't born with big teeth—it grew baby teeth first, which were replaced by its huge adult teeth later in life.

Unlike modern big cats, male and female
saber-toothed cats were about the same size.

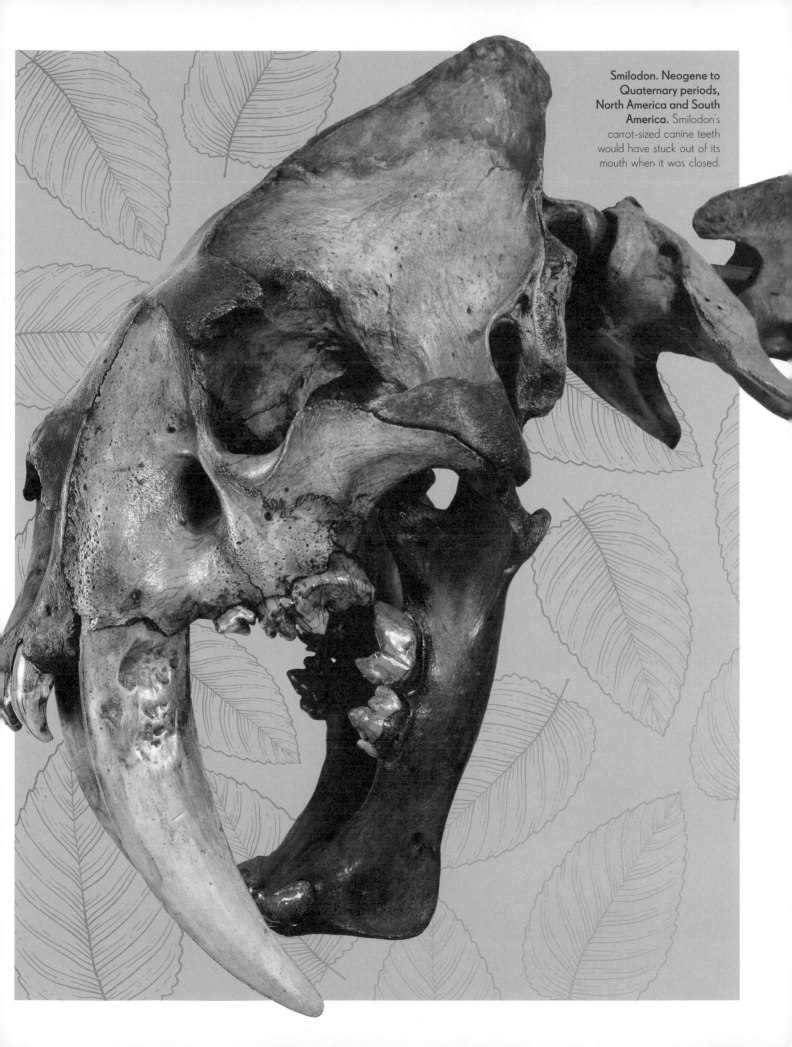

Smilodon. Neogene to Quaternary periods, North America and South America. Smilodon's carrot-sized canine teeth would have stuck out of its mouth when it was closed.

Thylacoleo

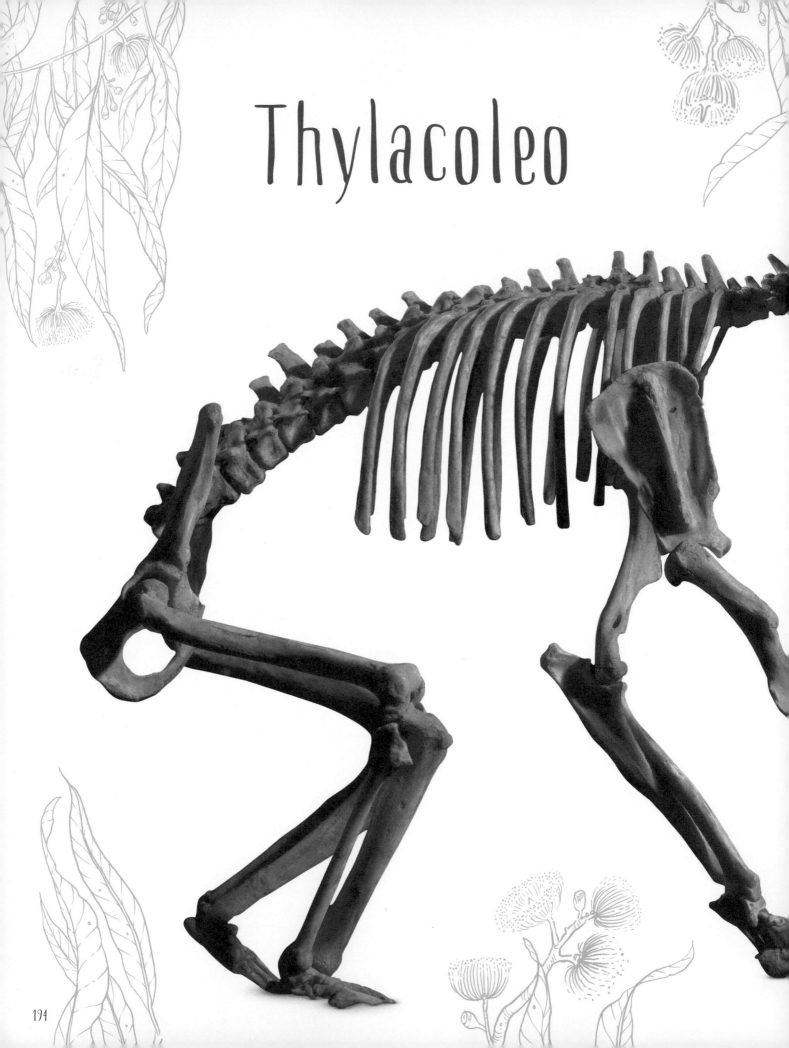

Despite its name, which means "pouch lion," Thylacoleo (THIGH-lah-coe-LEE-oh) was unrelated to lions. It was actually a marsupial, and it carried its young in a pocket on its belly, like kangaroos and koalas do. Its resemblance to a lion is due to the fact that Thylacoleo was adapted to a similar lifestyle and habitat—and it was a fearsome predator! Prowling the forests of Quaternary Australia, it was equipped with vicious, slicing teeth. Rather than the sharp canine teeth of other mammals, it was Thylacoleo's incisors that were sharp to stab prey. It also had retractable claws that could be hidden or extended, and its extra-large thumb claw was a deadly weapon.

For its size, Thylacoleo had the strongest bite of any mammal that has ever lived.

Thylacoleo. Quaternary Period, Oceania.
Thylacoleo had a short body with strong arms and powerful jaws. Fossils show that it existed from around 2 million years ago to 40,000 years ago.

Procoptodon

This giant kangaroo was taller than most humans—Procoptodon (pro-COP-toe-don) stood around 10 ft (2 m) tall and was the biggest and heaviest kangaroo that has ever existed. It roamed around Australia until about 15,000 years ago, across hot deserts and open forests. Procoptodon's massive size meant that it may not have been able to hop like modern-day kangaroos, and instead might have walked on two legs. Another difference from kangaroos today was its two elongated fingers, complete with curved claws, which were useful for pullling branches close to its mouth. However, like its relatives now, Procoptodon was a marsupial and carried its young in a snug pouch on its belly.

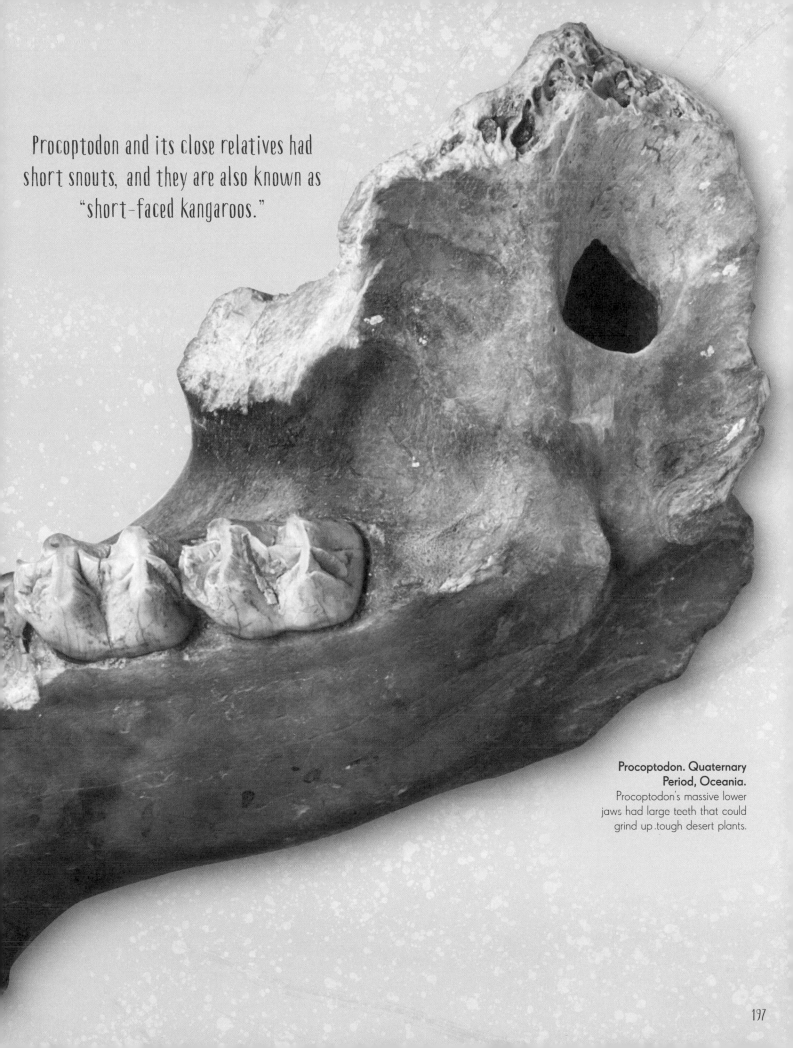

Procoptodon and its close relatives had short snouts, and they are also known as "short-faced kangaroos."

Procoptodon. Quaternary Period, Oceania.
Procoptodon's massive lower jaws had large teeth that could grind up tough desert plants.

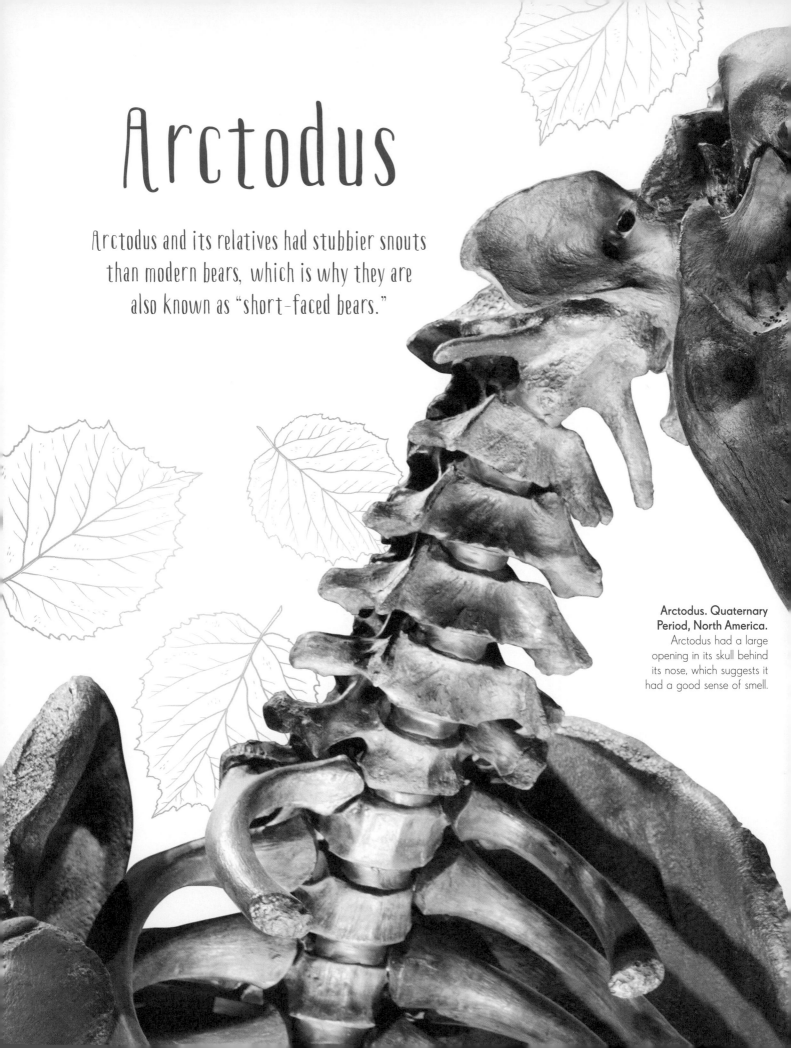

Arctodus

Arctodus and its relatives had stubbier snouts than modern bears, which is why they are also known as "short-faced bears."

Arctodus. Quaternary Period, North America. Arctodus had a large opening in its skull behind its nose, which suggests it had a good sense of smell.

Bigger even than a polar bear, 2-million-year-old Arctodus (ARK-toe-duss) was one of the largest bears in history. It had scary pointed teeth, but recent research suggests that it was probably an omnivore that ate any food it came across, from plants and fruit, to small animals and the remains of prey killed by other predators.

Around 3 million years ago, the continents of North and South America, which had previously been separated, became joined. This meant animals and plants could move easily between the two, and "The Great American Interchange" began. Short-faced bears were one of the animals which made the long journey to South America, and their descendants—spectacled bears—are still found there today.

Mylodon

There are a few surprising things about ground sloths, such as Mylodon (MY-low-don), when compared with modern sloths. First, they lived on the ground, not in trees. Some dug large burrows with their long, sharp claws. The main difference, however, was their size. Ground sloths were enormous. Sloths today weigh about 11 lb (5 kg), but Mylodon grew to more than 1.1 tons (1 metric ton)!

Discoveries of well-preserved Mylodon skin and dung confused early explorers into thinking that they belonged to a living animal, but most ground sloths became extinct by the end of the Ice Age. One population survived in the Caribbean until around 5,000 years ago, but, like previous ground sloths, these animals died out, possibly because of hunting by humans.

The giant ground sloth Megatherium
was as big as an elephant!

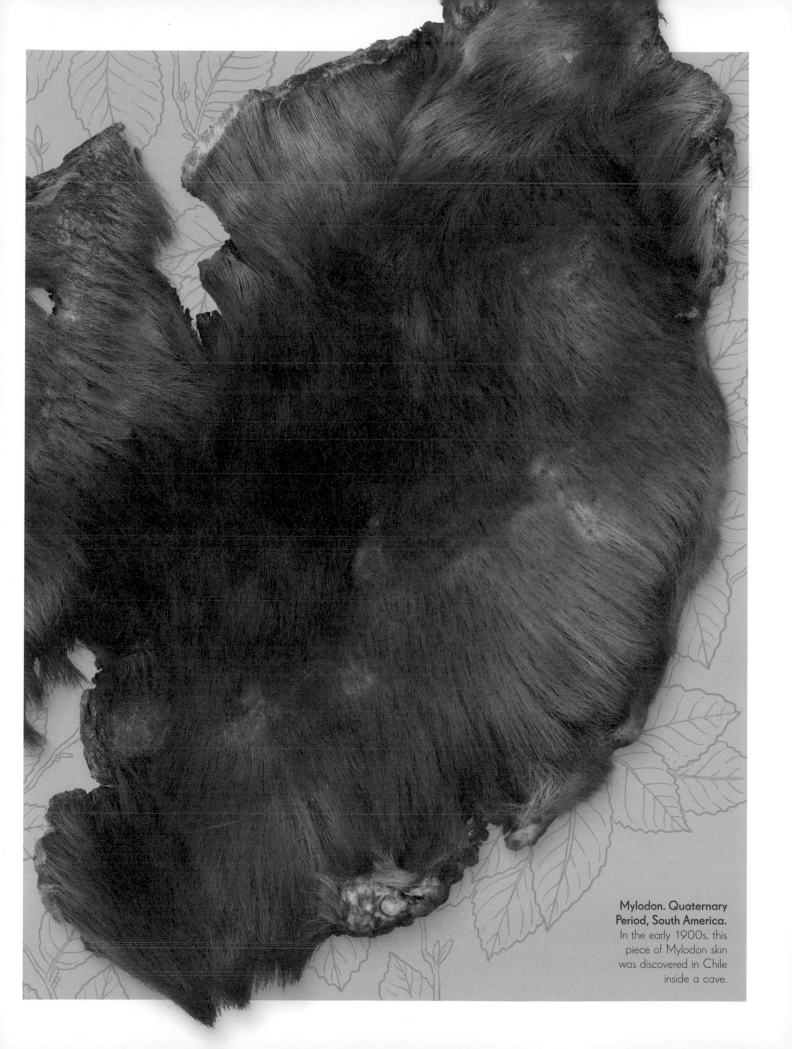

Mylodon. Quaternary Period, South America. In the early 1900s, this piece of Mylodon skin was discovered in Chile inside a cave.

Palaeoloxodon falconeri

The skulls of Palaeoloxodon falconeri may have inspired the myth of the one-eyed giants, called Cyclopses.

Elephants are the largest land animals today, but a miniature version, Palaeoloxodon falconeri (PAY-lee-oh-LOCKS-oh-don FAL-con-ER-ee) once lived on the islands of Sicily and Malta in the Mediterranean. Even when fully grown, these elephants were only about the size of a big dog! They became small to adapt to island living, where there wasn't enough space or food to support lots of large animals. It is thought that Palaeoloxodon falconeri was descended from prehistoric European elephants that were about 13 ft (4 m) tall. These ancestors reached the Mediterranean islands during the Ice Age, when the sea levels were much lower. The fossils of other tiny elephants can be dated to as recently as 11,700 years ago.

Palaeoloxodon falconeri.
Quaternary Period, Europe.
Palaeoloxodon falconeri was the smallest elephant to ever exist.

Woolly mammoth

With its shaggy coat and curved tusks, the woolly mammoth is a well-known Ice Age animal. About the size of a modern African elephant, this giant roamed the cold northern regions of the Earth, using its tusks to dig for plants. Woolly mammoths were well-adapted to living in icy environments. They had double-layered fur coats, which helped insulate them, and a small tail and ears, which lost less heat in the cold.

Some woolly mammoths, including calves, have been discovered perfectly preserved in ice. Most mammoths became extinct at the end of the Ice Age, about 10,500 years ago, mainly due to hunting by humans. Prehistoric people ate mammoth meat and even built shelters out of their huge bones.

Woolly mammoth. Quaternary Period, Asia, Europe, and North America. The curved tusks of woolly mammoths could reach 14 ft (4.2 m) long—the length of a small car.

A small population of woolly mammoths survived on an Arctic island until 3,700 years ago—after the ancient Egyptians had built the pyramids.

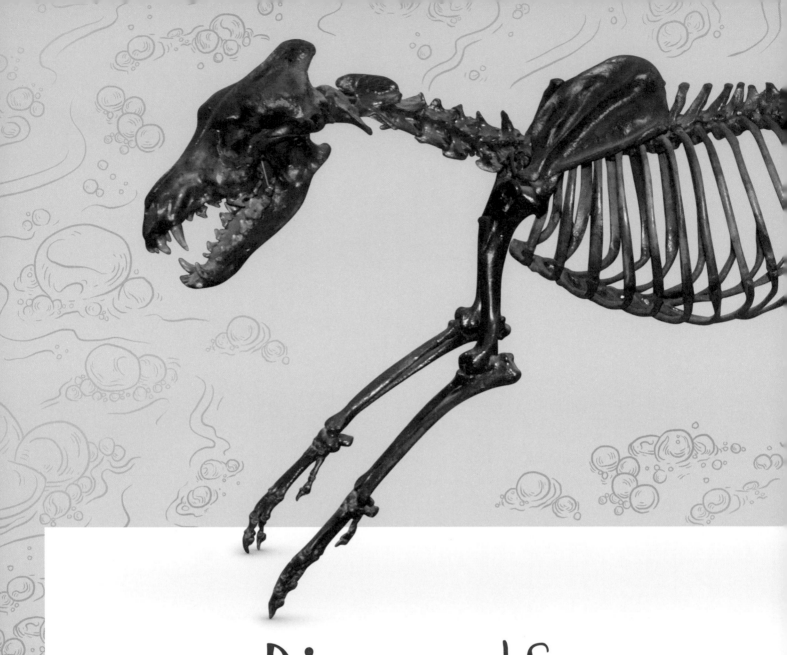

Dire wolf

Dire wolf fossils are often found close together, which suggests they lived and hunted in packs.

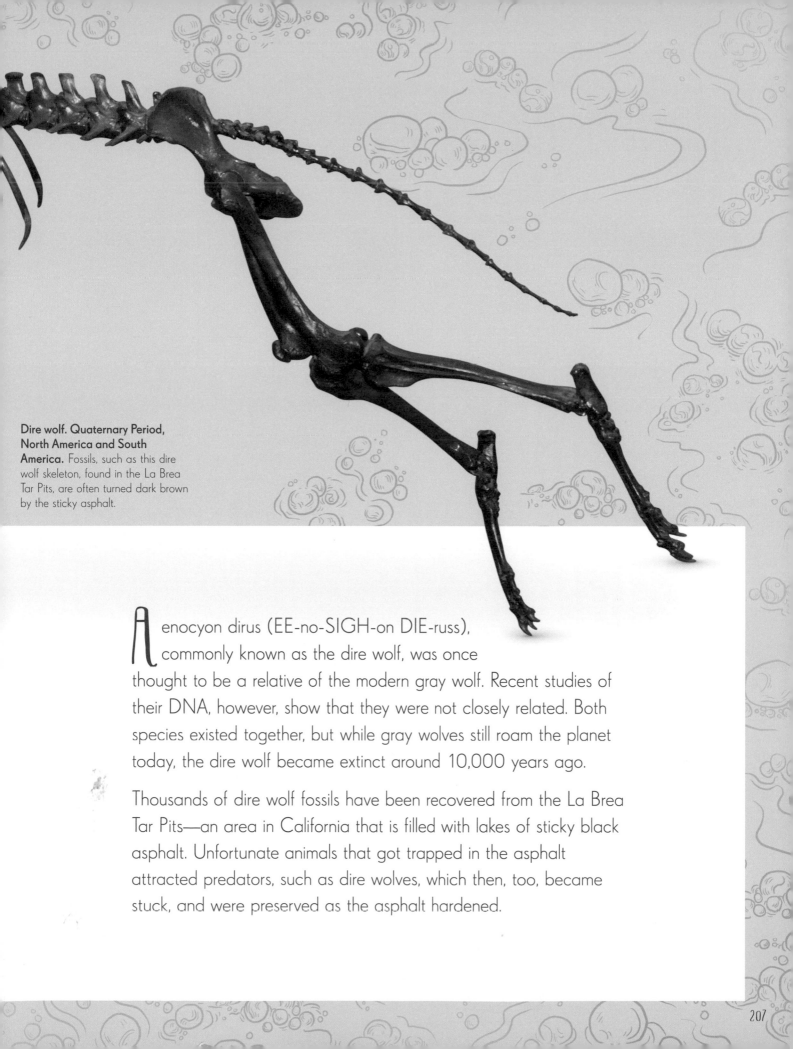

Dire wolf. Quaternary Period, North America and South America. Fossils, such as this dire wolf skeleton, found in the La Brea Tar Pits, are often turned dark brown by the sticky asphalt.

Aenocyon dirus (EE-no-SIGH-on DIE-russ), commonly known as the dire wolf, was once thought to be a relative of the modern gray wolf. Recent studies of their DNA, however, show that they were not closely related. Both species existed together, but while gray wolves still roam the planet today, the dire wolf became extinct around 10,000 years ago.

Thousands of dire wolf fossils have been recovered from the La Brea Tar Pits—an area in California that is filled with lakes of sticky black asphalt. Unfortunate animals that got trapped in the asphalt attracted predators, such as dire wolves, which then, too, became stuck, and were preserved as the asphalt hardened.

Great auk

The great auk was a penguinlike bird that lived on the northern Atlantic coasts. Humans hunted it for its downy feathers, which were stuffed into pillows. It became extinct in 1852.

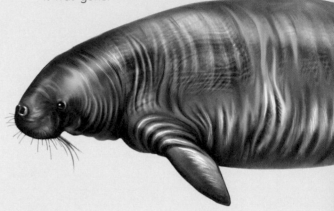

Steller's sea cow

Steller's sea cow was an aquatic mammal related to elephants. It lived in the northern Pacific Ocean, but people hunted it for its meat and fatty blubber. By 1768, it was gone.

Recently extinct

This book is filled with weird and wonderful plants and animals from Earth's past, but why aren't they still around today? Sometimes, species become extinct—that means every individual has died and there are no more left. A series of mass extinction events, when many species became extinct at the same time, have happened during the history of the Earth, including the asteroid strike that wiped out the non-bird dinosaurs. However, over time, other factors can cause extinction, too, such as a changing climate, hunting, and the destruction of a natural habitat. Here are several animals that have disappeared in recent history.

Passenger pigeon

Passenger pigeons were once found in their millions in North America, but over time their habitat was destroyed and many were hunted by people. By the early 1900s, they had disappeared completely.

Dodo

The dodo was a type of large pigeon, but it couldn't fly. When sailors arrived on the island of Mauritius, where it lived, they introduced rats, cats, and other animals that destroyed its nests. It became extinct at the end of the 17th century.

Thylacine

Also known as the Tasmanian tiger, the thylacine was a marsupial that looked like a wolf. It once lived across Oceania, but it was hunted by humans. The last known individual died in 1936.

Tree of life

Over the long history of the Earth, there have been all sorts of amazing and unusual plants and animals. Many no longer exist, but they are the ancestors of the organisms that live on the land and in the water today. This tree of life shows how closely the life-forms in this book are related to each other and how many belong to groups that are still around today.

Mammals
After the extinction of the non-bird dinosaurs, mammals grew bigger and spread across the Earth. The largest mammmal of all time, the blue whale, exists today.

Armadillos

Sloths

Odd-toed hoofed mammals

Carnivores

Elephants

Primates

Marsupials

Whales

Even-toed hoofed mammals

Amphibians

Amphibians
Living on land and in water, amphibians were the first four-legged animals to exist. They can't live far from fresh water though, as they need it to lay their eggs in.

Invertebrates
Invertebrates are animals without a backbone. They don't have a bony skeleton, but many have shells to protect their soft bodies. The first animals were aquatic invertebrates.

Bivalves

Echinoderms

Corals

Belemnites

Ammonites

Trilobites

Centipedes and millipedes

Microscopic life
The earliest life-forms on Earth were tiny organisms with one cell each, such as bacteria. Some types grew larger, such as nummulites, which could be the size of a small plate.

Nummulites

Eurypterids

Insects

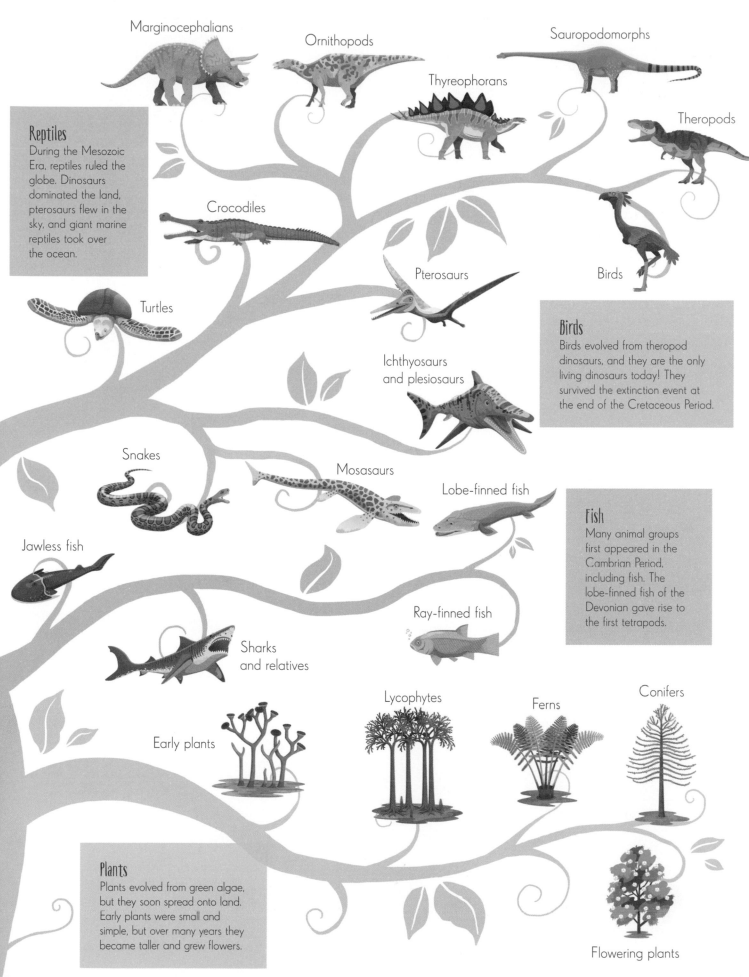

Marginocephalians

Ornithopods

Sauropodomorphs

Thyreophorans

Theropods

Reptiles
During the Mesozoic Era, reptiles ruled the globe. Dinosaurs dominated the land, pterosaurs flew in the sky, and giant marine reptiles took over the ocean.

Crocodiles

Turtles

Pterosaurs

Birds

Birds
Birds evolved from theropod dinosaurs, and they are the only living dinosaurs today! They survived the extinction event at the end of the Cretaceous Period.

Ichthyosaurs and plesiosaurs

Snakes

Mosasaurs

Lobe-finned fish

Fish
Many animal groups first appeared in the Cambrian Period, including fish. The lobe-finned fish of the Devonian gave rise to the first tetrapods.

Jawless fish

Ray-finned fish

Sharks and relatives

Lycophytes

Ferns

Conifers

Early plants

Plants
Plants evolved from green algae, but they soon spread onto land. Early plants were small and simple, but over many years they became taller and grew flowers.

Flowering plants

Pronunciations

Aenocyon dirus
EE-no-SIGH-on DIE-russ
Terrible wolf

Allosaurus
AL-oh-SORE-us
Different lizard

Anomalocaris
a-NOM-a-low-CAR-iss
Unlike other shrimp

Araucaria mirabilis
ah-row-CARE-ee-a
MIR-ah-BILL-iss
From Arauco, wonderous

Araucarioxylon
a-ROCK-air-EE-ox-i-lon
From Arauco forest

Archaeopteris
ar-kee-OP-ter-iss
Ancient fern

Archaeopteryx
ar-kee-OP-ter-ix
Ancient wing

Archaeotherium
ar-kee-oh-THEER-ee-um
Ancient beast

Archelon
ARE-chuh-lon
Ruling turtle

Arctodus
ARK-toe-duss
Bear tooth

Arthropleura
arth-row-PLOO-ra
Jointed rib

Australaster
OSS-tra-LAST-er
Southern star

Australopithecus
OSS-tra-low-PITH-ee-cuss
Southern ape

Aviculopecten
a-VIK-you-low-PECK-ten
Scallop

Basilosaurus
ba-SILL-oh-SORE-us
King lizard

Bison antiquus
BYE-son an-TIK-yoo-uss
Old bison

Calamites
CAL-a-MIGHT-eez
Reed

Cephalaspis
SEFF-a-LASP-iss
Head shield

charophyte
CAR-oh-fite
Unknown root plant

Coelodonta
see-loh-DON-ta
Hollow tooth

Confuciusornis
con-FEW-shus-OR-niss
Confucius bird

Confucius was a
Chinese philosopher.

Cooksonia
COOK-so-NEE-ah
Named after Ms. Cookson

Cryolophosaurus
cry-o-LOAF-o-SORE-us
Cold crested lizard

Deinocheirus
DINO-ky-russ
Terrible hand

Deltoblastus
DELL-toe-blas-tuss
Unknown

Dickinsonia
dickin-SO-nee-a
Named after Mr. Dickinson

Dimetrodon
die-MET-roe-don
Two measures of teeth

Diplodocus
dip-LOD-oh-kus
Double beam

Bones in Diplodocus's tail had
two long projections, or "beams"
on them.

Dunkleosteus
dun-kel-OSS-tee-uss
Named after Mr. Dunkle

Edmontosaurus
ed-MONT-oh-SORE-us
Edmonton lizard

Edmonton is a city in Canada.

Elasmosaurus
el-LAZZ-moe-SORE-us
Thin-plated lizard

Eodromaeus
EE-oh-drom-ay-uss
Dawn runner

Erbenochile
er-BEN-oh-CHILL-ee
Unknown

Eryops
EH-ree-ops
Drawn-out face

Euoplocephalus
YOU-owe-plo-SEFF-ah-lus
Well-armored head

Eurypterus
you-RIP-terruss
Broad paddle

Eusthenopteron
YOOS-then-OP-ter-on
Good strong fin

Florissantia
FLOOR-i-SAN-tee-a
From Florissant

Florissant is a town in
Colorado.

Giraffatitan
ji-RAF-a-TIE-tan
Giant giraffe

Glyptodon
GLIP-toe-don
Grooved tooth

Gomphotherium
GOM-foe-THEE-ree-um
Welded beast

Gomphotherium's lower
tusks were joined, or
"welded" together.

Haikouichthys
HIGH-koo-IK-this
Haikou fish

Haikou is a city in China.

Hallucigenia
ha-lucy-JEAN-ee-a
Wandering of the mind

Helicoprion
HELL-ee-coe-PRY-on
Spiral saw

Heliobatis
he-lee-oh-BAT-iss
Sun ray

Heliophyllum
he-lee-oh-FIE-lum
Sun leaf

Herrerasaurus
heh-RARE-ra-SORE-uss
Named after Mr. Herrera

Hesperornis
HESS-per-ORE-niss
Western bird

Ichthyostega
ICK-thee-oh-STAY-gah
Roofed fish

Iguanodon
ig-GWAH-no-don
Iguana tooth

Kentrosaurus
KEN-troh-SORE-us
Spike lizard

Lepidodendron
leppy-doe-DEN-dron
Scale tree

Lepidotes
leppy-DOE-tees
Scaly

Liopleurodon
LIE-oh-PLOOR-oh-don
Smooth-sided teeth

Magnolia
mag-NOH-lee-a
Named after Mr. Magnol

Maiasaura
MY-a-SORE-a
Good mother lizard

Massospondylus
MASS-oh-SPON-dill-us
Longer vertebrae

Mene
MEE-nee
Strong

Meganeura
MEGA-new-ra
Large-nerved

Meganeura had large veins,
or "nerves" on its wings.

Morganucodon
MORE-gan-oo-CODE-on
Glamorgan tooth

Glamorgan is an area in
Wales, UK.

Muttaburrasaurus
MOO-tah-BUH-ruh-SORE-us
Muttaburra lizard

Muttaburra is a town
in Australia.

Mylodon
MY-loh-don
Molar tooth

Neohibolites
NEE-oh-HIB-oh-lights
Unknown

Nummulite
NUM-you-light
Little coin

Opabinia
OH-pa-BIN-ee-a
From Opabin

Opabin Pass is found
in Canada.

Ornithomimus
OR-nith-oh-MIME-us
Bird mimic

Otodus megalodon
oh-TOE-dus MEG-a-loh-don
Ear-shaped tooth, big tooth

Oviraptor
OVE-ee-rap-tor
Egg thief

Oxynoticeras
OCK-see-no-TEE-ser-rass
Sharp-backed horn

Pachycephalosaurus
PACK-ee-SEFF-ah-low-SORE-us
Thick-headed lizard

Palaeoloxodon falconeri
*PAY-lee-oh-LOCKS-oh-don
fal-kon-EH-ree*
Ancient elephant

Panthera spelaea
pan-THEER-a SPEH-lee-a
Cave big cat

Parasaurolophus
PA-ra-SORE-oh-LOAF-us
Near crested lizard

*"Near" refers to its
similarity to another
dinosaur—Saurolophus.*

Patagotitan
pat-AG-oh-tie-tan
Patagonia giant

Phorusrhacos
for-uss-RA-koss
Bearer of wrinkles

Plioplatecarpus
PLY-oh-PLAT-ee-CAR-pus
More flat wrist

Polacanthus
POLE-a-CAN-thus
Many thorns

Procoptodon
pro-COP-toe-don
Forward hill tooth

Psittacosaurus
si-tak-a-SORE-us
Parrot lizard

Pterodactylus
TEH-roe-DACK-till-us
Winged finger

Sarcosuchus
sar-coe-SOO-kuss
Flesh crocodile

Smilodon
SMILE-oh-don
Scalpel tooth

Sciadophyton
SIGH-a-DOH-fite-on
Shadow plant

Seymouria
see-MOR-ee-a
From Seymour

Seymour is a city in Texas.

Sinosauropteryx
SIGH-no-sore-OP-ter-ix
Chinese winged lizard

Spinosaurus
SPINE-oh-SORE-us
Spine lizard

Stegosaurus
STEG-oh-SORE-us
Roofed lizard

Stenopterygius
sten-OP-terr-IDGE-ee-us
Narrow fin

Stromatolite
stroh-MA-toh-lite
Layered rock

Styracosaurus
sty-RACK-oh-SORE-us
Spiked lizard

Therizinosaurus
THERRY-zin-oh-SORE-us
Scythe lizard

Thylacoleo
THIGH-lah-coe-LEE-oh
Pouch lion

Tiktaalik
tik-TAA-lick
Large, freshwater fish

Titanoboa
tie-TAN-oh-BO-ah
Giant boa

Todites
toe-DIE-teez
Named after Mr. Tode

Triceratops
try-SERRA-tops
Three-horned face

Tyrannosaurus
tie-TAN-oh-SORE-us
Tyrant lizard

Uinatheirum
WIN-tah-THEE-ree-um
Uinta beast

The Uinta Mountains are
in the United States.

Velociraptor
vel-OSS-ee-RAP-tor
Swift seizer

Wiwaxia
we-WAX-ee-a
From Wiwaxy

The Wiwaxy Peaks are
in Canada.

Yi
yee
Wing

Glossary

ammonite Type of extinct ocean invertebrate with a shell. Most ammonites had coiled shells, but some were straight or wiggly

amphibian Vertebrate animal whose young live in water but which can live on land as an adult. The first amphibians appeared around 370 million years ago

ape Large primate without a tail

aquatic Description of an organism that lives in watery environments, such as rivers, lakes, and seas

arthropod Type of invertebrate that has a body divided into segments and jointed parts, such as insects, eurypterids, and trilobites

bird Vertebrate animal that has feathers and a beak. The first birds appeared around 160 million years ago. Birds are the only dinosaurs alive today

bivalve Type of invertebrate with two hinged shells and a soft body

canine tooth Pointed tooth found in the jaws of mammals used to grip, stab, and tear food. In some animals the canine teeth have become large tusks

carnivore Organism that eats only meat

climate Weather in an area over a long time

crest Feature found on the head of some animals. Crests are used to show off to mates and can be brightly colored

dinosaur Type of reptile whose name means "terrible lizard." Dinosaurs hold their legs directly beneath their bodies and lay hard-shelled eggs. Birds are dinosaurs

era Division of time that lasts for many millions of years. Eras can be further divided into periods

evolution Process of a species changing over a long period of time, until it is so different a new species is created

extinction Dying out of a species. When an organism becomes extinct there are no more of that organism left

fish Vertebrate animal that has fins and scales and that lives in water. The first fish appeared around 530 million years ago

fossil Preserved remains or traces of past life-forms. Body fossils are the bones, skin, and other parts of an organism, and trace fossils show footprints, dung, burrows, or other evidence of life

fossilization Process of becoming a fossil. This includes the burial of an organism and its preservation as it turns to rock over millions of years. Usually only the hard parts of an organism become fossils

frill Large, bony sheet that extended from the back of the skull of certain ceratopsians, such as Triceratops. Frills may have been brightly colored, and some had spikes sticking out of them

gastrolith Stone, found inside the stomach, that helps an animal with digestion

gill Organ found in aquatic animals that allows them to take in oxygen from the water in which they live

herbivore Animal that eats only plants

ice age Time when much of the Earth is covered by ice. The last ice age is known as the "Ice Age"

ichthyosaur Type of extinct reptile whose name means "fish lizard." Ichthyosaurs lived in the ocean and many looked like dolphins

incubation Process of keeping an egg warm so the baby animal inside can grow

insect Type of arthropod that has six jointed legs, and a body divided into a head, thorax, and abdomen. Many have wings and can fly

invertebrate Animal that does not have a backbone

larva Young of certain animals that undergo metamorphosis. Larvae, such as tadpoles, look very different from their adult form

lung Organ found in land-living animals that allows them to take in oxygen from the air

mammal Vertebrate animal that has hair, and feeds its young with milk. The first mammals appeared around 225 million years ago

marsupial Type of mammal that carries its young in a pouch

mass extinction event Short space of time when many different species become extinct; for example, when the non-bird dinosaurs were wiped out by an asteroid at the end of the Cretaceous Period

metamorphosis Process of an animal changing into a different form as it grows, such as a caterpillar becoming a butterfly

microscopic Description of something so tiny that it can only be seen using a microscope

migration Process of an animal traveling a long distance from one region to another, usually to find new food sources or to breed

mollusk Type of invertebrate with a soft body, such as squid, ammonites, and bivalves. Many have a protective outer shell

mosasaur Type of extinct ocean reptile with a short neck, large head, and flippers

mummified Description of the preserved soft parts of an organism, such as skin

nocturnal Description of an animal that is active at night

omnivore Animal that eats both plants and other animals

organism Living thing; for example, a plant or animal

osteoderm Bone found in the skin of an animal that helps to protect it from attack. Ankylosaurs had many osteoderms that formed shields on their backs

paleontologist Scientist who studies prehistoric life-forms

period Division of time that lasts for millions of years. Many periods make up an era

pigment Substance that gives something color

photosynthesis Process of a plant using the energy from sunlight to make food

plesiosaur Type of extinct ocean reptile with flippers. Some had very long necks

pliosaur Type of extinct ocean reptile with a short neck, large head, and flippers. Pliosaurs were a type of plesiosaur

pollination Process of pollen being moved from the male parts of a flower to the female parts of a flower, allowing the plant to make seeds. Pollen is often moved by animals called pollinators, such as bees

predator Animal that kills other animals for food

prehistoric Time before any written information exists

preserve Keep something in its original form without it rotting and decaying

prey Animal that a predator kills for food

pterosaur Type of extinct flying reptile with batlike wings. Pterosaurs are often called "pterodactyls"

reptile Vertebrate animal with scaly skin, such as dinosaurs, turtles, and snakes. The first reptiles appeared around 310 million years ago

resin Sticky substance made by some trees when they are damaged

species Group of organisms of the same type. Members of a species can reproduce together

spore Tiny reproductive structure made by plants and fungi that can grow into a new individual

tetrapod Animal with four limbs

trilobite Type of extinct arthropod whose body is divided lengthwise into three lobes

tusk Long tooth that sticks out of the mouth of some mammals

vertebra Bone from the backbone of an animal

vertebrate Animal with a backbone

Visual guide

Billion Years Ago (BYA); Million Years Ago (MYA); Years Ago (YA)

Stromatolite, page 6
Group: Bacteria
Height: 3 ft (1 m)
Location: Worldwide
Period: Precambrian to present
Time: 3.5 BYA—present

Dickinsonia, page 8
Group: Invertebrate
Length: 5 ft (1.5 m)
Location: Asia, Europe, Oceania
Period: Precambrian
Time: 567–550 MYA

Anomalocaris, page 10
Group: Invertebrate
Length: 3 ft (1 m)
Location: Asia, North America, Oceania
Period: Cambrian
Time: 520–500 MYA

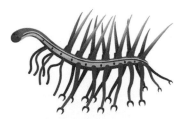

Hallucigenia, page 14
Group: Invertebrate
Length: 2 in (5 cm)
Location: Asia and North America
Period: Cambrian
Time: 510 MYA

Cooksonia, page 16
Group: Plant
Height: 1 in (2.5 cm)
Location: Worldwide
Period: Silurian to Devonian
Time: 433–393 MYA

Eurypterus, page 18
Group: Invertebrate
Length: 24 in (60 cm)
Location: North America
Period: Silurian
Time: 432–418 MYA

Australaster, page 20
Group: Invertebrate
Length: 1 in (2.5 cm)
Location: Oceania
Period: Silurian
Time: 430 MYA

Cephalaspis, page 22
Group: Fish
Length: 10 in (25 cm)
Location: Europe and North America
Period: Devonian
Time: 400 MYA

Erbenochile, page 24
Group: Invertebrate
Length: 2 in (5 cm)
Location: Africa
Period: Devonian
Time: 400 MYA

Archaeopteris, page 26
Group: Plant
Height: 80 ft (24 m)
Location: Worldwide
Period: Devonian to Carboniferous
Time: 385-323 MYA

Heliophyllum, page 28
Group: Invertebrate
Height: 6 in (15 cm)
Location: Africa, North America,
and South America
Period: Devonian
Time: 380 MYA

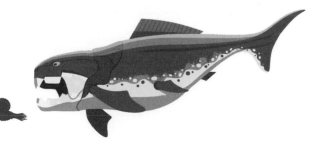

Dunkleosteus, page 30
Group: Fish
Length: 30 ft (9 m)
Location: Worldwide
Period: Devonian
Time: 380–360 MYA

Tiktaalik, page 32
Group: Fish
Length: 9 ft (2.7 m)
Location: North America
Period: Devonian
Time: 375 MYA

Ichthyostega, page 34
Group: Fish
Length: 5 ft (1.5 m)
Location: North America
Period: Devonian
Time: 370–360 MYA

Aviculopecten, page 38
Group: Invertebrate
Length: 6 in (15 cm)
Location: Worldwide
Period: Devonian to Triassic
Time: 360–200 MYA

Lepidodendron, page 40
Group: Plant
Height: 165 ft (50 m)
Location: Worldwide
Period: Carboniferous
Time: 360–300 MYA

Calamites, page 42
Group: Plant
Height: 165 ft (50 m)
Location: Worldwide
Period: Carboniferous
Time: 350–300 MYA

Arthropleura, page 44
Group: Invertebrate
Length: 8 ft (2.5 m)
Location: Europe and North America
Period: Carboniferous
Time: 320–299 MYA

Meganeura, page 46
Group: Invertebrate
Wingspan: 3 ft (1 m)
Location: Europe
Period: Carboniferous
Time: 305–299 MYA

Deltoblastus, page 48
Group: Invertebrate
Body height: 1 in (2.5 cm)
Location: Asia
Period: Permian
Time: 298–252 MYA

Dimetrodon, page 50
Group: Mammal ancestor
Length: 15 ft (4.6 m)
Location: Europe and North America
Period: Permian
Time: 295–272 MYA

Seymouria, page 52
Group: Amphibian
Length: 24 in (60 cm)
Location: Europe and North America
Period: Permian
Time: 290–275 MYA

Helicoprion, page 54
Group: Fish
Length: 33 ft (10 m)
Location: Worldwide
Period: Permian
Time: 280–270 MYA

Todites, page 56
Group: Plant
Height: 3 ft (1 m)
Location: Asia and Europe
Period: Permian to Jurassic
Time: 260–160 MYA

Araucarioxylon, page 60
Group: Plant
Height: 200 ft (60 m)
Location: North America
Period: Triassic
Time: 250 MYA

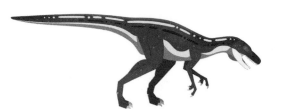

Herrerasaurus, page 62
Group: Reptile
Length: 20 ft (6 m)
Location: South America
Period: Triassic
Time: 230 MYA

Morganucodon, page 66
Group: Mammal
Length: 4 in (10 cm)
Location: Asia and Europe
Period: Triassic to Jurassic
Time: 205–180 MYA

Oxynoticeras, page 68
Group: Invertebrate
Length: 31 in (80 cm)
Location: Europe and North America
Period: Jurassic
Time: 200–190 MYA

Cryolophosaurus, page 70
Group: Reptile
Length: 21 ft (6.5 m)
Location: Antarctica
Period: Jurassic
Time: 194–188 MYA

Massospondylus, page 72
Group: Reptile
Length: 20 ft (6 m)
Location: Africa
Period: Jurassic
Time: 190 MYA

Stenopterygius, page 74
Group: Reptile
Length: 13 ft (4 m)
Location: Europe
Period: Jurassic
Time: 185–170 MYA

Lepidotes, page 76
Group: Fish
Length: 12 in (30 cm)
Location: Worldwide
Period: Jurassic to Cretaceous
Time: 180–94 MYA

Liopleurodon, page 78
Group: Reptile
Length: 23 ft (7 m)
Location: Europe
Period: Jurassic
Time: 166–155 MYA

Araucaria mirabilis, page 80
Group: Plant
Height: 330 ft (100 m)
Location: South America
Period: Jurassic
Time: 160 MYA

Yi, page 82
Group: Reptile
Wingspan: 24 in (60 cm)
Location: Asia
Period: Jurassic
Time: 159 MYA

Allosaurus, page 84
Group: Reptile
Length: 33 ft (10 m)
Location: North America
Period: Jurassic
Time: 156–150 MYA

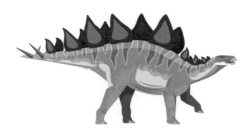

Stegosaurus, page 86
Group: Reptile
Length: 30 ft (9 m)
Location: Europe and North America
Period: Jurassic
Time: 155-150 MYA

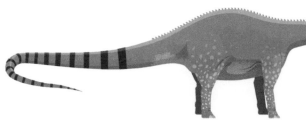

Diplodocus, page 90
Group: Reptile
Length: 85 ft (26 m)
Location: North America
Period: Jurassic
Time: 155-150 MYA

Pterodactylus, page 92
Group: Reptile
Wingspan: 3 ft (1 m)
Location: Europe
Period: Jurassic
Time: 155–148 MYA

Kentrosaurus, page 94
Group: Reptile
Length: 16 ft (5 m)
Location: Africa
Period: Jurassic
Time: 152 MYA

Archaeopteryx, page 96
Group: Reptile
Length: 20 in (50 cm)
Location: Europe
Period: Jurassic
Time: 150 MYA

Sarcosuchus, page 98
Group: Reptile
Length: 31 ft (9.5 m)
Location: Africa and South America
Period: Cretaceous
Time: 133–112 MYA

Polacanthus, page 100
Group: Reptile
Length: 16 ft (5 m)
Location: Europe
Period: Cretaceous
Time: 130–125 MYA

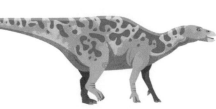

Iguanodon, page 102
Group: Reptile
Length: 40 ft (12 m)
Location: Europe
Period: Cretaceous
Time: 125 MYA

Psittacosaurus, page 106
Group: Reptile
Length: 6½ ft (2 m)
Location: Asia
Period: Cretaceous
Time: 125–120 MYA

Confuciusornis, page 108
Group: Bird
Length: 20 in (50 cm)
Location: Asia
Period: Cretaceous
Time: 125–120 MYA

Sinosauropteryx, page 110
Group: Reptile
Length: 3 ft (1 m)
Location: Asia
Period: Cretaceous
Time: 120 MYA

Muttaburrasaurus, page 112
Group: Reptile
Length: 23 ft (7 m)
Location: Oceania
Period: Cretaceous
Time: 110–100 MYA

Neohibolites, page 114
Group: Invertebrate
Length: 6 in (15 cm)
Location: Worldwide
Period: Cretaceous
Time: 100 MYA

Patagotitan, page 116
Group: Reptile
Length: 102 ft (31 m)
Location: South America
Period: Cretaceous
Time: 100–95 MYA

Magnolia, page 120
Group: Plant
Height: 100 ft (30 m)
Location: Worldwide
Period: Cretaceous to present
Time: 100 MYA—present

Spinosaurus, page 122
Group: Reptile
Length: 53 ft (16 m)
Location: Africa
Period: Cretaceous
Time: 99–94 MYA

Hesperornis, page 124
Group: Bird
Length: 6 ft (1.8 m)
Location: North America
Period: Cretaceous
Time: 84–78 MYA

Elasmosaurus, page 126
Group: Reptile
Length: 33 ft (10 m)
Location: North America
Period: Cretaceous
Time: 80 MYA

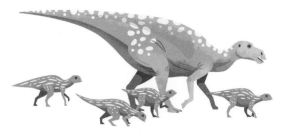

Maiasaura, page 128
Group: Reptile
Length: 30 ft (9 m)
Location: North America
Period: Cretaceous
Time: 77 MYA

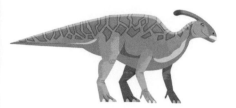

Parasaurolophus, page 130
Group: Reptile
Length: 31 ft (9.5 m)
Location: North America
Period: Cretaceous
Time: 76 MYA

Euoplocephalus, page 132
Group: Reptile
Length: 18 ft (5.5 m)
Location: North America
Period: Cretaceous
Time: 76–74 MYA

Ornithomimus, page 134
Group: Reptile
Length: 11 ft (3.5 m)
Location: North America
Period: Cretaceous
Time: 76–66 MYA

Velociraptor, page 136
Group: Reptile
Length: 6½ ft (2 m)
Location: Asia
Period: Cretaceous
Time: 75 MYA

Archelon, page 138
Group: Reptile
Length: 15 ft (4.6 m)
Location: North America
Period: Cretaceous
Time: 75 MYA

Styracosaurus, page 140
Group: Reptile
Length: 18 ft (5.5 m)
Location: North America
Period: Cretaceous
Time: 75 MYA

Oviraptor, page 144
Group: Reptile
Length: 5 ft (1.5 m)
Location: Asia
Period: Cretaceous
Time: 75–71 MYA

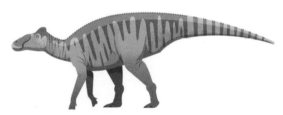

Plioplatecarpus, page 146
Group: Reptile
Length: 18 ft (5.5 m)
Location: Europe and North America
Period: Cretaceous
Time: 73–68 MYA

Edmontosaurus, page 148
Group: Reptile
Length: 40 ft (12 m)
Location: North America
Period: Cretaceous
Time: 73–66 MYA

Deinocheirus, page 150
Group: Reptile
Length: 36 ft (11 m)
Location: Asia
Period: Cretaceous
Time: 70 MYA

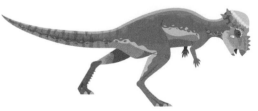

Pachycephalosaurus, page 152
Group: Reptile
Length: 13 ft (4 m)
Location: North America
Period: Cretaceous
Time: 70–66 MYA

Triceratops, page 154
Group: Reptile
Length: 30 ft (9 m)
Location: North America
Period: Cretaceous
Time: 68–66 MYA

Tyrannosaurus, page 156
Group: Reptile
Length: 43 ft (13 m)
Location: North America
Period: Cretaceous
Time: 68–66 MYA

Nummulite, page 160
Group: Single-celled organism
Length: 6 in (16 cm)
Location: Worldwide
Period: Paleogene to present
Time: 66 MYA—present

Titanoboa, page 162
Group: Reptile
Length: 43 ft (13 m)
Location: South America
Period: Paleogene
Time: 60–58 MYA

Heliobatis, page 164
Group: Fish
Length: 35 in (90 cm)
Location: North America
Period: Paleogene
Time: 55–48 MYA

Mene, page 166
Group: Fish
Length: 12 in (30 cm)
Location: Worldwide
Period: Paleogene to present
Time: 55 MYA—present

Florissantia, page 168
Group: Plant
Flower length: 2 in (5 cm)
Location: North America
Period: Paleogene
Time: 52–23 MYA

Basilosaurus, page 170
Group: Mammal
Length: 65 ft (20 m)
Location: Africa and North America
Period: Paleogene
Time: 41–33 MYA

Uintatherium, page 172
Group: Mammal
Length: 13 ft (4 m)
Location: Asia and North America
Period: Paleogene
Time: 40 MYA

Archaeotherium, page 174
Group: Mammal
Length: 6½ ft (2 m)
Location: North America
Period: Paleogene
Time: 34–25 MYA

Gnat in amber, page 176
Group: Invertebrate
Length: ½ in (8 mm)
Location: Europe
Period: Paleogene
Time: 30 MYA

Phorusrhacos, page 178
Group: Bird
Height: 8 ft (2.5 m)
Location: South America
Period: Neogene
Time: 20–13 MYA

Megalodon, page 180
Group: Fish
Length: 59 ft (18 m)
Location: Worldwide
Period: Neogene
Time: 16–3.6 MYA

Gomphotherium, page 182
Group: Mammal
Height: 10 ft (3 m)
Location: Africa, Asia, Europe, and North America
Period: Neogene
Time: 13–5 MYA

Australopithecus, page 184
Group: Mammal
Height: 5 ft (1.5 m)
Location: Africa
Period: Neogene
Time: 4–2 MYA

Coelodonta, page 186
Group: Mammal
Length: 13 ft (4 m)
Location: Asia and Europe
Period: Neogene to Quaternary
Time: 4 MYA—10,000 YA

Glyptodon, page 190
Group: Mammal
Length: 10 ft (3 m)
Location: North America and South America
Period: Neogene to Quaternary
Time: 3 MYA—12,000 YA

Smilodon, page 192
Group: Mammal
Length: 6½ ft (2 m)
Location: North America and South America
Period: Neogene to Quaternary
Time: 2.5 MYA—10,000 YA

Thylacoleo, page 194
Group: Mammal
Length: 5 ft (1.5 m)
Location: Oceania
Period: Quaternary
Time: 2 MYA—40,000 YA

Procoptodon, page 196
Group: Mammal
Height: 6½ ft (2 m)
Location: Oceania
Period: Quaternary
Time: 2 MYA—15,000 YA

Arctodus, page 198
Group: Mammal
Height: 6 ft (1.8 m)
Location: North America
Period: Quaternary
Time: 2 MYA—11,000 YA

Mylodon, page 200
Group: Mammal
Length: 10 ft (3 m)
Location: South America
Period: Quaternary
Time: 1.8 MYA—10,000 YA

Palaeoloxodon falconeri, page 202
Group: Mammal
Height: 3 ft (1 m)
Location: Europe
Period: Quaternary
Time: 800,000 YA

Woolly mammoth, page 204
Group: Mammal
Length: 13 ft (4 m)
Location: Asia, Europe, and North America
Period: Quaternary
Time: 200,000—3,700 YA

Dire wolf, page 206
Group: Mammal
Length: 5 ft (1.5 m)
Location: North America and South America
Period: Quaternary
Time: 125,000—10,000 YA

Project editor Olivia Stanford
Project art editors Charlotte Jennings, Roohi Rais
US Senior editor Shannon Beatty
US editor Margaret Parrish
Publishing coordinator Issy Walsh
Senior jacket designer Elle Ward
Senior production editor Rob Dunn
Production controller Basia Ossowska
Picture researcher Rituraj Singh
DTP Designers Syed Mohammad Farhan,
Sachin Gupta
Managing editor Jonathan Melmoth
Managing art editors Diane Peyton Jones,
Ivy Sengupta
Deputy art director Mabel Chan
Creative director Helen Senior
Publishing director Sarah Larter

Consultant Dr. Dean Lomax

First American Edition, 2021
Published in the United States by DK Publishing
1450 Broadway, Suite 801, New York, NY 10018

Copyright © 2021 Dorling Kindersley Limited
DK, a Division of Penguin Random House LLC
21 22 23 24 25 10 9 8 7 6 5 4 3 2 1
001–323295–Sept/2021

A catalog record for this book
is available from the Library of Congress.
ISBN 978-0-7440-3943-6

DK books are available at special discounts when purchased
in bulk for sales promotions, premiums, fund-raising, or educational
use. For details, contact: DK Publishing Special Markets,
1450 Broadway, Suite 801, New York, NY 10018
SpecialSales@dk.com

Printed and bound in China

For the curious
www.dk.com

224

The author would like to thank her son Altay Y. Turan for comments and discussion.
DK would like to thank: Katie Lawrence and Kathleen Teece for editorial assistance;
Polly Goodman for proofreading; Lynne Murray for picture library assistance; Daniel Long
for the species illustrations; Angela Rizza for the pattern and cover illustrations; and the
Chinese Academy of Sciences, the Great North Museum, Museum de Toulouse, Museum
of Paleontology in Tübingen, and Royal Ontario Museum for their kind permission to use
their fossil photographs.

About the author:
Professor Anusuya Chinsamy-Turan is an
award-winning, world-renowned paleobiologist
from South Africa—and an expert on the
microscopic structure of bones of prehistoric and
modern animals. She has written both academic titles
and children's books on dinosaurs and other prehistoric
life, and is a committed science communicator.